The Apalachee Indians
and Mission San Luis

Native Peoples, Cultures, and Places of the
Southeastern United States

Jerald T. Milanich, General Editor

Each volume in this series is intended to provide a highly
readable overview of an American Indian group, the culture
of a discrete period, region or place, a major archaeological
site, or a specific topic of interest crossing many cultures. The
goal is to make readers aware of the native American heritage
of the southeastern United States.

The Apalachee Indians and Mission San Luis by John H. Hann
and Bonnie G. McEwan

Florida's Indians: From Ancient Times to the Present by
Jerald T. Milanich

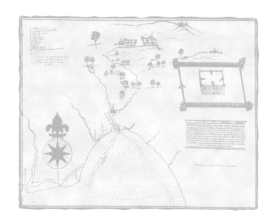

The Apalachee Indians and Mission San Luis

John H. Hann and Bonnie G. McEwan

UNIVERSITY PRESS OF FLORIDA

Gainesville · Tallahassee · Tampa · Boca Raton

Pensacola · Orlando · Miami · Jacksonville

This publication has been financed in part with historic preservation grant assistance provided by the Bureau of Historic Preservation, Division of Historical Resources, Florida Department of State, assisted by the Historic Preservation Advisory Council. However, the contents and opinions do not necessarily reflect the views and opinions of the Florida Department of State, nor does the mention of trade names or commercial products constitute endorsement or recommendation by the Florida Department of State.

 A Florida Heritage Publication

Book & Cover Design by Synergy Design Group.

Printed in Hong Kong on acid-free paper. All rights reserved

03 02 01 00 99 98 6 5 4 3 2 1

Library of Congress Cataloging-in-Publication Data
Hann, John H.
The Apalachee Indians and Mission San Luis / John H. Hann and
Bonnie G. McEwan
p. cm.—(Native peoples, cultures, and places of the southeastern United States)
Includes bibliographical references and index.
ISBN 0–8130–1564–2 (cloth: alk. paper).
ISBN 0–8130–1565–0 (pbk.: alk. paper)
1. San Luis de Apalachee Site (Fla.) 2. Apalachee Indians—History. 3. Apalachee Indians—Missions. 4. Apalachee Indians—Antiquities. 5. Missions, Spanish—Florida—Tallahassee Region—History. 6. Florida—History—Spanish colony, 1565–1763. 7. Tallahassee Region (Fla.)—Antiquities. I. McEwan, Bonnie G. (Bonnie Gair), 1954–. II. Title. III. Series.
E99.A62H37 1998 97–23341
975.9'8801—dc21

The University Press of Florida is the scholarly publishing agency for the State University System of Florida, comprising Florida A&M University, Florida Atlantic University, Florida International University, Florida State University, University of Central Florida, University of Florida, University of North Florida, University of South Florida, and University of West Florida.

University Press of Florida
15 Northwest 15th Street
Gainesville, FL 32611

http://nersp.nerdc.ufl.edu/ ~ upf

For our families

CONTENTS

FOREWORD

It is a great pleasure to help bring the story of Mission San Luis to readers through the new Florida Heritage series of books. During the first two centuries of its history as a European colony, Florida was under Spanish rule. The Spanish Crown and the Catholic Church together brought European ways of life to Florida and other colonies with a system of mission settlements. San Luis was the principal mission town of Apalachee Province in the Florida panhandle, serving as both the administrative and the religious capital of a chain of missions stretching from St. Augustine.

In 1983, the State of Florida, through its Conservation and Recreation Lands Program, acquired fifty acres of Mission San Luis. Under the ground, suggested only by the faintest dips and rises of the grassy lawn, were the archaeological remains of the center of the seventeenth-century town. The Department of State began in 1983 a program of archaeological and historical research accompanied by museum interpretation to learn about life in Spanish Florida and to bring that story to the public. Now, nearly fifteen years later, Mission San Luis is an archaeological park and outdoor museum with reconstructed buildings, exhibits, guided tours, and educational programs.

The story of San Luis presented here has been developed by painstaking archaeological excavations at the site as well as through translations of seventeenth- and eighteenth-century documents from Spanish archives. It is the most thoroughly documented and archaeologically investigated mission in the Southeast. We now know how the town center was laid out, where the church, cemetery, council house, fort, and some houses were located, how many people lived here, and we even know some of them by name and reputation.

Drawing on this research, the wonderful illustrations presented in this book were created during development of the outdoor exhibits at San Luis. The exhibits, three years in the making, are now installed at San Luis thanks to the continuing support of the National Endowment for the Humanities. San Luis is one of the few missions in Spanish Florida interpreted for the public and the only site of its kind where a living history program is being developed.

I hope you enjoy the story of San Luis and I invite you to visit us in Tallahassee and experience for yourself the fascinating story of the Native American and Spanish people who lived together in Florida for more than two centuries.

Sandra B. Mortham
Secretary of State

PREFACE

Our American Indian legacy is a rich and important part of our country's heritage. The history of native peoples in the Americas dates back at least 12,000 years; in 1492 thousands of tribes and millions of people lived all across North and South America.

In the 500 years following Christopher Columbus's initial voyage to the Bahamas and the Caribbean, American Indians suffered mightily. Many Indian groups disappeared. Others survived the depredations of the past, and today their descendants have a brighter future. The stories of all these people—past and present—deserve to be told.

One such story is the focus of the first book in this new series. The Apalachee Indians played a major role in the geopolitics of the seventeenth and early eighteenth centuries.

If one could select the most knowledgeable historian and the most knowledgeable archaeologist to write a book about the Apalachee Indians and Mission San Luis, everyone's first choices would be John Hann and Bonnie McEwan, authors of this volume. These scholars have worked long, hard, and successfully to discover new information about the native peoples of Florida's eastern panhandle and their participation in the Spanish colonial system.

The Apalachee Indians and Mission San Luis, a joint endeavor of the University Press of Florida and the Florida Division of Historical Resources, illustrates the rewards of interdisciplinary research and interagency cooperation.

Jerald T. Milanich
Series Editor

ACKNOWLEDGMENTS

First and foremost we thank the Florida Legislature and Florida's Conservation and Recreation Lands Program, both of which had leaders with the vision to purchase San Luis and maintain support for research and education staff over the years. As part of the Florida Department of State's Division of Historical Resources, we are indebted to Secretary of State Sandra B. Mortham and Division Director George W. Percy for their encouragement and support.

Generous grants for interpretive planning (GM-24665-92) and implementation (GM-25295-95) from The National Endowment for the Humanities provided the inspiration for the book. Over the years, we have benefitted from the counsel of many valued colleagues, including Henry Baker, Ronald Wayne Childers, Ann Cordell, Kathleen Deagan, Richard Ehrlich, Michael Gannon, Jane Landers, Clark Spencer Larsen, Eugene Lyon, Rochelle Marrinan, Jerald Milanich, James Miller, Jeffrey Mitchem, Lee Newsom, Nicholas Paffett, Elizabeth Reitz, John Sallas, Margaret Scarry, and Herschel Shepard.

Synergy Design Group, under the direction of partners John LoCastro and Mary Frances Weathington, designed and produced the layout and digital art. Many of the book's illustrations are John's original art created for interpretive panels at San Luis. Leigh Thompson and Dave McGowan are responsible for the final versions of the maps and much of the digital coloring, and they contributed significantly to the book's prepress production. Many thanks also go to Lillian Cliff, Synergy's office manager, whose organization and attention to detail kept their staff on task.

Among the other artists involved with the project, none is finer than Edward Jonas. His artistic genius is readily apparent, and we are extremely grateful for his involvement. Other talented artists from the Museum of Florida History who worked on various graphics and design elements are Robert Deaton, Lynn Rogers, and Bill Celander.

We also owe a great debt to our predecessors who established the research foundation at San Luis and kept interest in the site alive. Mark F. Boyd, an avocational historian, was the first person to transcribe and translate documents specifically related to San Luis. Archaeological research was initiated by John W. Griffin (1948), followed by Hale G. Smith (1950), Charles H. Fairbanks (1956–1957), and San Luis's first full-time archaeologist, Gary Shapiro (1984–1988).

Many archaeologists have worked on field and lab crews at San Luis over the years, and all have made their own unique contributions. However, our current staff members—Jerry Lee, Jonathan Gray, and Heidi Broadfield—are among the best ever. They have helped with the book in countless ways, from pulling artifacts to be photographed to proofing the manuscript.

We thank staff members Elyse Cornelison and Charles Poe for generating digitized maps for the book. Lois Markham and Mable Revell gave us considerable logistical support. Our editor at the press, Judy Goffman, provided insightful comment and recommendations, while Jean Wilson assisted with word processing and formatting.

Jerald T. Milanich provided the initial encouragement to develop and submit our manuscript to this new popular series under his editorship. And, finally, James J. Miller, state archaeologist and chief of the Bureau of Archaeological Research, has been our mentor, collaborator, and colleague through the years, and all of our achievements are, in large part, due to him.

Our sincere thanks to everyone.

INTRODUCTION

This book was written for the many visitors, educators, volunteers, and general public with an interest in the Apalachee Indians, the impact of missionization on the native population, and Mission San Luis in particular. It is based on fifteen years of historical and archaeological research, even more if we count our predecessors back to the 1940s.

We have intentionally designed this book to be of interest to a broad audience, but we encourage those desiring more information to consult the publications listed in the back.

In great part the book is the fruit of four years of generous support by the National Endowment for the Humanities to develop a variety of new media to interpret the site for the public. This endeavor required a tremendous amount of graphic development which was guided by our research. Several talented artists translated our often fragmentary and technical findings into exceptional works of art, and we impress on the reader that, in this instance, a picture truly is worth a thousand words.

In the interests of clarity and consistency, we have maintained a uniform spelling of native place-names that appear on the maps and in the text. That uniformity will be preserved even in the presentation of formal lists of villages, ignoring the departures from the norm that occur on those lists.

We hope that this volume will give people a greater appreciation of Florida history, particularly the tumultuous seventeenth century. It has always been our overarching goal to investigate this final episode of the Apalachee Indians in their traditional homeland as thoroughly as possible. We have also been concerned with the Spaniards who resided in the area and the nature of their interaction with the Apalachee. In many respects we still have much to learn, but we hope that you will enjoy reading about our discoveries as much as we have enjoyed making them.

J.H.H.
B.G.M.

CHAPTER 1

Apalachee Province and the First Europeans

As Hernando de Soto's forces crossed the Aucilla River in 1539 into the land of the Apalachee, fierce warriors with "skin painted all over with red ochre and with their heads full of multicolored feathers" attempted to block their advance. All along the trails de Soto had followed since his landing in Tampa Bay, he and his men had heard "many praises and wonders" about this province as "a very large one with an abundance of maize and warriors who would riddle them with arrows, butcher them, burn and destroy them." Eleven years earlier, natives in Tampa Bay told another Spanish expedition that they would find gold in Apalachee along with other things that the Spaniards valued. The tales of gold and silver and of a large province proved untrue, but the soldiers did find an abundance of maize and other foods along with fierce and unrelenting opposition, which burned the name Apalachee into their memories.

Apalachee men were known to wear body paint during raids and ball games.

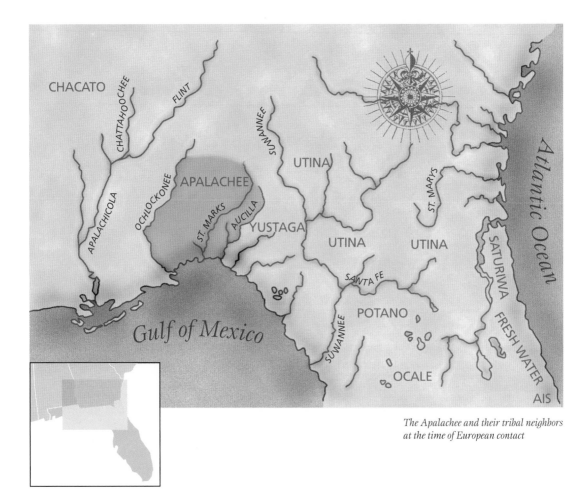

The Apalachee and their tribal neighbors at the time of European contact

Apalachee Province in the early sixteenth century was a densely populated yet geographically small Indian chiefdom. It occupied an area bounded by the Aucilla River to the east and the Ochlockonee River to the west and extended from approximately the Georgia state line to the Gulf of Mexico. Apalachee's settlements were confined largely to what is today Leon and Jefferson counties. The upland region's red clay soils were among the most fertile in Florida and presented ideal conditions for successful agriculture. The province's many lakes and ponds, along with the swampy St. Marks lowlands, provided abundant aquatic resources. The Gulf coastal waters were also regularly exploited by the Apalachee for seafood.

The tales of gold and other wealth, and of a large and powerful people, may have been an afterglow from an earlier, glorious time. Prior to European contact, the Apalachee chiefdom was the the only true Mississippian culture in Florida. Its people raised many of the same crops, such as maize, beans, and squash, as the Mississippian societies of the interior Southeast, and they built ceremonial centers with platform mounds, plazas, and villages. Their premier ceremonial mound center was located at Lake Jackson.

The Apalachee had highly stratified social, political, and religious organizations, and they shared elements of a regional belief system. They also participated in an extensive exchange network that included manufactured symbolic items and raw materials.

The Apalachee chiefdom may have been perceived as bigger and more important than it was because of its trade network and possible alliances with other important mound centers stretching north through Georgia and Alabama and westward into the Mississippi Valley and Oklahoma. Because of that misperception, European mapmakers gave the Apalachee's name to the Appalachian Mountains.

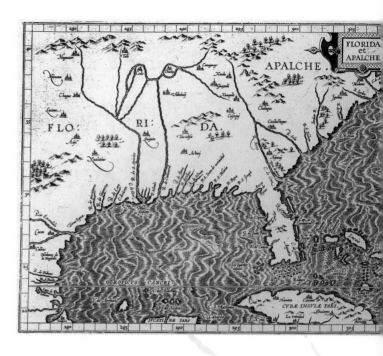

*Sixteenth-century maps by Corneille Wytfliet (1597) (**above**) and Diego Gutiérrez (1562) (**below**) show Apalachee Province associated with mountains far north of its actual location.*

European Contact

Although Alonso Álvarez de Pineda sailed along the coast of Apalachee in 1519, the first Europeans recorded as having established contact with Apalachee's people arrived almost a decade later. Pánfilo de Narváez brought forces into Apalachee territory in 1528, as did Hernando de Soto eleven years later. Narváez landed in Tampa Bay, and, despite a language barrier, the local natives communicated to him that he would find the riches he sought among the Apalachee to the north. With scant wisdom and little food, Narváez dismissed his ships and marched overland to Apalachee. His hopes of finding a second Mexico with a wealth of gold and silver were not realized. That disappointment, along with the fierce hostility he met from the Apalachee and the illnesses he and many of his men experienced, caused them to abandon the enterprise. They attempted to reach Mexico in improvised boats built by his men on Apalachee's coast.

De Soto landed in Tampa Bay in 1539 and shortly thereafter also headed for Apalachee. With greater wisdom than that exercised by Nárvaez, he ordered his ships to remain in Tampa Bay until he sent them instructions about a rendezvous.

The Apalachee's reputation for bellicosity and military prowess must have preserved them from major incursions by neighboring peoples. The absence of fortifications around Apalachee village centers when the first Europeans arrived suggests that they felt relatively secure against all but small-scale raids directed at outlying population clusters. Despite the military disparity between the two sides during the armed incursions into Apalachee by Narváez and de Soto, the Apalachee lived up to their reputation as fierce warriors. During de Soto's five-month presence in their territory, the Apalachee harassed him and his men constantly. But, despite the excellence of the Apalachee long bow and their guerrilla-style attacks, the two sides were mismatched technologically and tactically. For all the advances of their culture, the Apalachee were facing unfamiliar firearms, the powerful crossbow, and other weapons of iron and steel, but the greatest disparity was the Spaniards' possession of cavalry. In all but heavy woods, cavalry gave the Spaniards an insuperable advantage against anything but an unrelenting assault by waves of warriors, which was not a tactic any of Florida's natives would have considered.

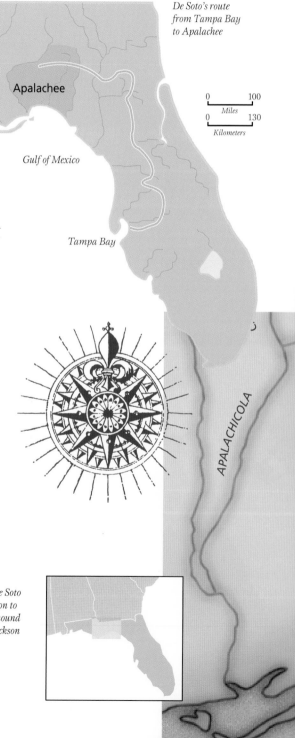

De Soto's route from Tampa Bay to Apalachee

Apalachee

0   100
Miles
0   130
Kilometers

Gulf of Mexico

Tampa Bay

APALACHICOLA

Major villages encountered by de Soto in 1539 in relation to the abandoned mound center at Lake Jackson

THE APALACHEE CHIEFDOM
IN THE SIXTEENTH CENTURY

By the time of the Apalachee's encounters with Narváez and de Soto, the paramount center at Lake Jackson had apparently been abandoned. The chroniclers of the de Soto expedition mentioned a number of villages, including Anhaica (also spelled Inihaica) and Ivitachuco. Anhaica and Ivitachuco were also the paramount villages at the beginning of the seventeenth century, when Spaniards next returned to Apalachee, and throughout the mission period. Ivitachuco was the eastern gateway to the province, immediately west of which de Soto found the land populous and possessing vast fields of maize, beans, and pumpkins.

The lowlands of the St. Marks River, which at that time extended north to Lake Miccosukee, were uninhabited. They effectively divided the province into eastern and western halves. Anhaica, where de Soto spent the winter of 1539–1540, lay in the western half. The de Soto chroniclers described Anhaica's chief as lord of the province. In view of the later identification of Ivitachuco's chief as the overall lord of the province in a time of peace, Anhaica's role as paramount center during de Soto's incursion was probably a consequence of its position as the head war town. That status is compatible with the ball game rivalry between the two towns and their competition on the chunkey field as well. They probably represented different moieties, or two groups divided by descent or location.

The site thought to be that of de Soto's Anhaica was identified in 1988 by B. Calvin Jones of the Florida Bureau of Archaeological Research. It was named the Martin site after former Florida governor John W. Martin, who once owned the property and built a home on it in the 1930s. The site is located just under four miles from Lake Jackson and less than a mile from the present-day Capitol. In view of the extensive territory covered by Apalachee villages in mission times, the Anhaica of de Soto's day could have

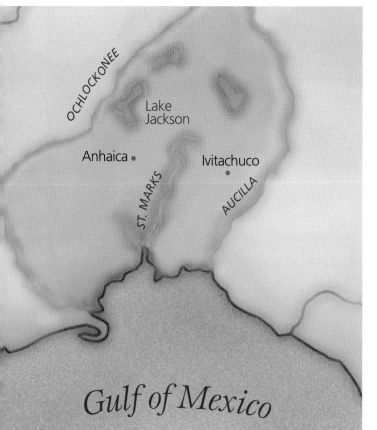

*This crossbow quarrel (**left**) and pieces of chain mail (**above**) were among many artifacts that enabled archaeologists to determine that Anhaica had a sixteenth-century Spanish component.*

Illustration of Hernando de Soto courtesy of State Photographic Archives, Florida Department of State, Division of Historical Resources.

embraced Tallahassee's "Capitol Hill" as well as the Martin site. The 1988 identification was based on the discovery of a number of early sixteenth-century artifacts, such as distinctive Spanish pottery, European beads and coins, a crossbow quarrel, chain mail, and pig remains. Documents identify crossbows, chain mail, and hogs as things that de Soto took on his expedition.

The discovery of the Anhaica site is particularly important for the archaeological glimpse it provides into Apalachee culture at the time of contact. Although subsistence apparently changed little from the time Lake Jackson was the capital, the pottery reveals a marked transition in external influences. By the early sixteenth century the ceramics began to look less like those from the Middle Mississippian chiefdoms to the northwest, with incised and punctated designs such as Fort Walton Incised, and more like those from the southern Appalachian Mississippian of the Georgia Piedmont with stamped designs, such as Lamar Complicated Stamped and Leon Check Stamped. The move from Lake Jackson to Anhaica also reflects the abandonment of mound building. However, if today's Capitol Hill was part of the Anhaica complex, the break with mound centers may not have been total. Three sides of the hill are steeply sloped and would have given it the appearance of a gigantic natural mound, thus retaining some of the symbolism associated with Lake Jackson.

The move from Lake Jackson to Anhaica may reflect a change in the ruling line, perhaps a consequence of the people's becoming dissatisfied with the demands for labor and other forms of tribute from the former ruling family. Growing ties with peoples from the Macon, Georgia, area and factional disputes within the power elite may also have brought the downfall of the late prehistoric rulers. Although we may never understand all of the factors that prompted this change, we know that from the time that the Lake Jackson ceremonial center was abandoned, Apalachee's relations with other mound centers to the west and northwest were disintegrating while contact with Macon area natives was on the rise.

EXPOSURE TO DISEASE

Although limited in duration, the Apalachee's first contacts with Spaniards were violent. Moreover, these first European *entradas* may have introduced invisible enemies that the Apalachee never saw. Death from disease took a far greater toll on the native population than the Spaniards' weapons. We do not know the population of Apalachee when Spaniards initially visited the province in 1528 and 1539, but the first Spanish estimates made in the early seventeenth century indicated that the population was between 30,000 and 36,000. If there had been any severe epidemics of newly introduced diseases in the sixteenth century, this estimate of the early 1600s suggests a minimum pre-epidemic population of 50,000 to 60,000. The introduction of diseases into areas where the indigenous people have no immunity can result in epidemics that reduce the population by as much as 50 percent. This trend would eventually become more acute with the establishment of missions and a Spanish garrison in Apalachee.

THE SPANIARDS' LOSS OF INTEREST IN APALACHEE

The Apalachee had given a most hostile reception to the two Spanish expeditions that invaded their territory in 1528 and 1539. For the rest of the sixteenth century there was no further contact between Apalachee and Spaniards except for a shipwrecked Spaniard whom the Calusa of Florida's southwest coast held as a slave. Whatever his contacts with the Apalachee may have been, the slave considered the Apalachee to be "the best Indians in Florida; superior to those of Tocobaga, Carlos, Ais, Tegesta," and the other groups he had encountered. We do not know for sure on what he based his judgmental comparison. Those he mentioned by name were largely or exclusively fisher-hunter-gatherers rather than sedentary agriculturalists like the Apalachee. He probably saw the Apalachee as offering the best prospect among Florida's native populations of being "civilized" in the European sense and of becoming Christianized. Similar observations were made by a friar who visited Apalachee in 1608. He noted that the province was "very populated" and that its people were more organized and refined than those on the coast with whom he was acquainted.

There is no record of any further contact between the Apalachee and Europeans for the rest of the sixteenth century following de Soto's departure from the province in March 1540. Spaniards who arrived at Pensacola Bay in 1559 to establish a settlement, and who soon lost most of their food supplies to a hurricane, gave no thought to reinvading Apalachee to relieve their hunger. Some of the colonists who had been with de Soto remembered all too well the harassment they had suffered at the hands of the Apalachee, so they traveled to Coosa in far northwest Georgia in their search for provisions. In the 1560s, a Frenchman stationed with René de Laudonnière at Fort Caroline traveled westward into the hinterland as far as Yustaga Province which bordered on Apalachee, but that was as close as any European is recorded as having come to Apalachee for the rest of the century.

Diseases introduced by Europeans had a profound impact on Florida's native populations.

The principal chief and a dancer at San Luis during a ceremony in the council house

APALACHEE SOCIETY

POLITICAL STRUCTURE

Like most Mississippian societies, the Apalachee were matrilineal. Lineages or groups of related individuals were combined into clans, and a person's clan membership was the same as his or her mother's. The Apalachee also were matrilocal. When a man married he went to live in the village of his wife's family, among whom he always remained something of an outsider.

Nobility and one's degree of elite status were based on genealogical proximity to the ruling family. However, beyond a few degrees of kinship from the royal family, an egalitarian clan structure prevailed. Three levels of chiefly power were recognized among the Apalachee: paramount, principal, and local. The most powerful Apalachee was the paramount chief who had authority over the entire province. During late prehistoric times, the head chief lived on top of one of the platform mounds at Lake Jackson. Implicit evidence from historic times suggests that the

Apalachee may have had dual leaders, a head peace chief and a head war chief, similar to their northern neighbors. Under that system the paramount peace chief ruled during times of peace, but in times of war supreme power passed to the paramount war chief. In later times, Anhaica's chief (paramount war chief) was identified as a brother of Ivitachuco's chief (paramount peace chief), although the relationship may have been fictive. Chiefs of many villages bore native names associated with the two paramount rulers, suggesting that family or clan ties bound many of the leaders together.

Beneath the paramount chiefs were provincial rulers whom Spaniards referred to as principal chiefs. Each chief's authority extended over a geographically defined area that included satellite villages; the village leaders were subject to the principal chief in whose jurisdiction they lived.

The *inija*, referred to by Spaniards at times as *mandador* or order-giver, was second in command to the principal chief. He also served as the chief's primary counsellor, as city

Lake Jackson mound center was the late prehistoric capital of Apalachee Province.

manager, and as stand-in for the chief in dealings with outsiders during periods of absence. In larger villages, the inija had a number of deputies known as *chacales* who directed the workers in the community fields. Inijas also seem to have been repositories of tribal lore and information on the succession to chieftainships.

Other members of the leadership circle and upper class included important warriors, shamans, other counsellors to the chief, the chiefs' families, and skilled ballplayers.

Conspicuously absent from mention is the nephew-heir destined to succeed the chief in Apalachee. Among the Guale of the Georgia coast that heir bore the title *tunaque* and enjoyed special powers and privileges even before becoming chief. Among those privileges was a reserved seat in the council house and participation in the deliberations held

The Apalachee treated their superior ballplayers like celebrities.

there. However, there is no evidence that the Apalachee heir held an equivalent position.

Apalachee chiefs and other leaders enjoyed certain privileges of office. The community provided for them; they controlled large stores of food-stuffs; they were entitled to booty captured on raids; they were exempt from manual labor and, during the mission period, exempt from demeaning punishments such as whipping. Chiefs had a right to all bear and panther skins obtained on lands under their jurisdiction or by their tribes-men. In prehistoric times paramount chiefs, members of his family, and possibly his servants or retainers were buried in one of the platform mounds with regalia of his office. After the Apalachee abandoned the mound centers, it is likely that chiefs and other important leaders continued to receive special treatment at death that set them apart from ordinary Indians.

Apalachee Rulers

The positions of chief and inija were hereditary. Under the matrilineal system this meant that upon the death of a chief, his position passed to the eldest son of his eldest sister rather than to his own son. However, one of the chief's biological sons enjoyed the title and position of usinulo, meaning "beloved son." The usinulo and the chief played a prominent role in rituals associated with the ball game, indicating that the chief and his family exercised both priestly and political power. There is no evidence that women ever attained chieftainships or other positions of authority in Apalachee, as they did among their Timucua neighbors to the east, but there is a suggestion that, when a chief lacked a son, a daughter might be named usinulo.

It is probable that the chiefly line of succession was not always adhered to rigidly when the deceased chief's eldest nephew by his eldest sister was distinctly not the most desirable heir in the line of succession. Upon the death of a chief, if legitimate heirs were not present to make their claims at once, ambitious men holding the reins of power might advance one of their own as heir. Attempts to oust a hereditary successor usually followed an active campaign of spreading false reports about the suitability of the absent heir or heirs. Such an instance was recorded for a minor chieftainship during the mission period when a visiting Spanish judge was presented with a rightful heir's claim. After the judge authenticated the legitimacy of his succession with native authorities, the heir was installed.

In Spanish times, at least, when lawful chiefs became incapable of ruling because of age or infirmity, native and Spanish authorities intervened to give the reins of power to another under the title of governor, while the lawful chief continued to retain his title. The nephew-heir often was the person to whom the title of governor was awarded.

BELIEF SYSTEMS

The belief system that late prehistoric Apalachee shared with other Mississippian societies is nowhere more apparent than at the paramount center at Lake Jackson. This platform mound complex originally consisted of seven large earthen mounds that are similar to those at other Mississippian sites. The shared warfare complex can be seen in the special insignia worn by and buried with chiefs at Lake Jackson, such as repoussé copper breastplates, engraved shell artifacts, and copper and stone celts. A "birdman dancer" design found on one of the copper breastplates from Lake Jackson incorporates birds of prey, commonly used as design elements by Mississippian peoples. Many of the artifacts recovered from the Lake Jackson center were manufactured outside of the area and are made from nonlocal materials. These objects were intended to identify chiefs, remind others of their power, and separate the elite from commoners. In contrast with the elaborate mound burials of the ruling class, commoners were most frequently buried in pits outside their houses.

Although the Apalachee were clearly linked to other Mississippian societies, they interacted with other groups as well. Evidence of other cultural contacts can be seen in the distribution of ceramic styles shared by the Apalachee among the natives of peninsular Florida and among those along the Gulf Coast of northwest Florida. The Apalachee ball game and its associated rituals were found among the linguistically distinct Timucua chiefdoms to the east as far away as the Gainesville area. But Mississippian chiefdoms immediately to the north of Apalachee in the Chattahoochee River Valley played a game that was distinct, at least in its use of a lacrosse-like stick that was absent in the Apalachee game. The Apalachee game's regalia and the absence of an instrument for propelling the ball have parallels in the game played by Indians of Oklahoma, the Southwest, and Mexico. The Apalachee game was referred to as "the younger brother of war." It shared the characteristic of being a substitute for war

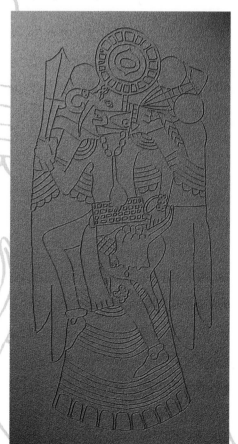

This decorative motif commonly referred to as the "birdman dancer" was found on a copper breastplate from Lake Jackson.

equally with its northern neighbors and others as far away as the Iroquois, who played stickball, and with the southwesterners and Mexicans whose game did not use an instrument.

LANGUAGE

The Apalachee were related linguistically to the speakers of the Muskhogean language family found to the north, northeast, and northwest of them in Georgia and Alabama rather than to their closest neighbors to the east, the Timucua speakers. In fact, the name *Apalachee* formed part of the name *Apalachicola,* which was used early in the historic era to designate most of the Hitchiti-speaking Indians (a Muskhogean language group) living on the Chattahoochee River. The Apalachicola are believed to be descendants of that river valley's early inhabitants in contrast to the linguistically distinct Coweta and Kasihta, who also lived there in the latter half of the seventeenth century. But despite those linguistic ties, the title of *mico* for head chief, which prevailed among the rest of the Muskhogean family, was not recorded among the Apalachee. Rather, the Apalachee used the chiefly title *holahta*, which was among several, including *cacique*, that the Timucua speakers used for principal chief.

DAILY LIFE

As with most southeastern Indians, there was a sharp division of labor between Apalachee men and women. Men fished, hunted, and cleared the fields for planting. They constructed all of the buildings and manufactured the tools and paraphernalia used in various activities and rituals. Men were warriors who defended their villages in raids by and against enemy tribes. They also played the Apalachee ball game and chunkey. With the expansion of planting that occurred under the mission regime as Apalachee began supplying provisions to St. Augustine and Havana, men began to participate in the cultivating and weeding of field crops. Most of the chores linked to the newly introduced animal husbandry were also assumed by men because of the similarity to hunting, but the care of chickens and possibly of hogs fell to the women.

Women were responsible for kitchen gardens and the field crops once they were planted. They also did most of the work connected with maintaining their homes, such as gathering foods, making pottery, and cooking. Women gathered most wild foods, cured animal skins, and collected firewood. Widows were often provided for from community fields in exchange for sweeping public areas such as the council house and plaza. Women also played a ball game, but it differed from the men's in that they used a short lacrosse-like instrument to propel the ball. A friar's remark suggests that women played their game only on rare occasions, noting that they did not have any regular form of entertainment other than dancing and that they spent all the rest of their time and energy in the service of their homes and families.

Although Apalachee men traditionally prepared the fields, women were largely responsibile for planting and tending them.

CHAPTER 2

Missions to the Apalachee

Early in the seventeenth century the attitude of some of the Apalachee leaders toward the European intruders changed sufficiently for them to send word to the Spanish governor at St. Augustine that the Apalachee were interested in rendering obedience to Spain's king and in receiving friars who would teach them the new faith brought by the Spaniards. They were but one of a number of Florida tribes that expressed such sentiments beginning in the second half of the 1590s.

We do not fully understand why so many native leaders began to have a change of heart during that period—leaders who, until then, were determined to have nothing to do with the Spaniards and were quick to show hostility against any who came into their territory. Some tribal leaders closer to St. Augustine than the Apalachee were influenced by newly converted native leaders with whom they maintained friendly relations. Others had a growing sense of Spain's power and a realization that the Spaniards had come to stay, so they decided that accommodation was at least in their interest, if not necessary.

Glass beads were among the most common and popular gifts given to the Florida natives by the Spaniards.

Native leaders' rendering of obedience to Spain's king was also influenced by the governors' distribution of gifts. Such gift-giving began earlier, but it was not officially approved by the Crown until 1593. The royal sanction and funding increased the scope and attractiveness of the gifts. As a consequence, a number of new chiefs established friendly relations with the Spaniards in 1597 upon the arrival of a new governor, Gonzalo Méndez de Canzo. Such occasions were the usual time for invitations to meet the governor. Some were from western Timucua provinces of north Florida's hinterland more or less adjacent to Apalachee. When the Apalachee saw a traditional enemy on their eastern borders making such an accommodation, they may have wanted to do the same to avoid having their enemy enlist Spanish power against them.

The Apalachee leaders who asked for friars may have lost faith in the native religious system and in its value as a bulwark for their political power. Many of the native leaders were high priests as well as chiefs. They used claims of special

Gun parts, lead shot, and gunflints have been recovered from both the chief's residence and the council house at San Luis.

ties with the divinities to legitimize the strong political authority that they already exercised or aspired to attain. That situation seems to have been tested with the arrival of the Europeans. The leaders' failure to cope with the epidemics that spread because Florida's natives had no immunity undoubtedly shook the people's faith in traditional beliefs. The appeal of the Spaniards' Christian God may have been enhanced considerably because the Spaniards seemed to be protected against the diseases that were killing off the natives.

Native leaders met in the council house every day to discuss community affairs.

In Lake Jackson times the rulers possessed exotic goods secured in trade with other mound centers, and the goods were a highly visible, legitimizing symbol of the leaders' claim to rule. During the mission period, native leaders acquired imported goods such as Spanish clothing, firearms, and iron tools, and these goods similarly served to enhance the prestige of the chiefs and relegitimize tarnished authority and diminished rank. The esoteric knowledge and skills such as reading and writing that friars made available to new converts had the same effect.

While it is impossible to determine the relative importance of these various factors, there is documentary evidence that the Apalachee leaders' request for friars was based in part on an expectation that a Spanish alliance would mean Spanish support. Such support would enable the leaders to regain the control over their subjects that had been lost. Awareness of that expectation and other considerations led Spanish authorities to delay establishment of the first formal missions in Apalachee for a quarter of a century. Despite the good relationship between the Apalachee and Spaniards brought about by a friar working in the western Timucua-speaking provinces of Potano and Utina in 1608, missionization efforts in Apalachee Province did not begin in earnest until 1633.

Friar reading to Indians. Oil painting by and copyright of Gil Cohen. Reproduced courtesy of the artist and the U.S. Department of the Interior, National Park Service, San Antonio Missions National Historical Park.

INITIAL MISSION EFFORTS, 1608–1633

Fray Martín Prieto established friendly relations between Spaniards and Apalachee to facilitate the friars' work among the western Timucua. As friars began an intensive effort to Christianize the Timucua provinces of Potano and Utina, Fray Prieto saw the region's chronic warfare with the Apalachee as an obstacle to the friars' work among the Timucua. Encouraged by the Apalachee's expression of a desire for friendship with the Spaniards, Fray Prieto went to

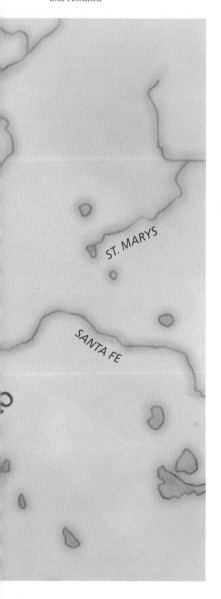

Illustration showing Utina, Potano, and Apalachee provinces as well as the Apalachee villages of Ivitachuco and Anhaica

Apalachee, accompanied by Utina Province's head chief in hopes of ending the warfare between the Apalachee and the Timucua. From the Yustaga village of Cotocochuni, Prieto sent two Apalachee whom the Timucua were holding there as prisoners. They were to explain to Apalachee's leaders the mission of peace that Prieto and western Timucua's head chief were bringing.

When Prieto reached Apalachee's easternmost village of Ivitachuco, which was the seat of Apalachee's paramount chief, he found the province's entire population led by seventy chiefs assembled there to greet him. He estimated the crowd at over 36,000. His peace mission was successful. In opening the conclave, Ivitachuco's seventy-year-old chief spoke at great length in favor of peace. Once the agreement was concluded, the chief addressed the assembly again, expressing his joy that peace had been established. After the participants had feasted, the assembled Apalachee chieftains appointed the chief of Anhaica to visit the governor at St. Augustine and render the province's obedience in their name.

Prieto remained in Apalachee only six days, confining his visit to Ivitachuco and a few other nearby settlements. But not long thereafter another friar named Alonso Serrano visited Apalachee and traveled more extensively through the province, preaching to the people and giving Christian names to many of the villages. Between 1608 and 1612, other friars followed, doing missionary work in an informal fashion. Both Prieto and Serrano composed accounts of their experiences in Apalachee, but these have not been found. Although a considerable number of Apalachee expressed a desire to become Christian at that time, twenty-five years would pass before the Spaniards established a formal permanent presence in the province.

A number of considerations caused this delay. One was opposition among some Apalachee to the friars' presence. Twice during the period 1608–1612 friars were forced to leave because the leaders who had invited them could not guarantee their safety. In deferring the establishment of missions there, Governor Juan Fernández de Olivera spoke in 1612 of the need for soldiers in a fortified post to lend support to the friars and control the unruliness of some of the Indians who did not obey their chiefs. Even if the use of soldiers had been feasible, Crown policy during this period expressly forbade military support during the initial work of evangelization in new territories.

Another major consideration was the massive task faced by the friars to complete the evangelization of the Guale and the Timucua-speaking provinces. Even more daunting was the problem of sending supplies to friars at such a long distance from St. Augustine. North Florida's river system did not lend itself to east-to-west transportation. Supplying even the western Timucuan missions posed serious problems. Whatever interest the governors may have had in extending the missions into Apalachee was probably tempered by the Apalachee leaders' lack of interest in sending men to work on Crown projects in St. Augustine and on outlying farms owned by soldiers. Once a chief gave obedience to the Crown, governors expected them to furnish such labor, but the independent Apalachee rejected this demand.

Nevertheless, Fray Lorenzo Martínez, superior of Florida's Franciscans, reported in 1612 that the friars visiting Apalachee were receiving warm appeals to establish a permanent presence there. When he told them that no friars were available, the Indians insisted that the friars set up a cross before leaving and indicate sites where they might build churches for when friars did become available. Dedication of the later Ivitachuco mission to San Lorenzo suggests that a church may have been built there in 1612 and that it was so named as a tribute to Lorenzo Martínez, who had lobbied the king in support of the immediate evangelization of Apalachee. San Francisco de Ocone is another village where a church may have been erected at the time. Its inhabitants claimed in 1657 that theirs was the first place in Apalachee in which Christianity had been established.

The friars likely continued transitory contacts on a reduced basis until the launching of the formal mission effort on October 16, 1633. Communication

probably became more frequent after friars began to work in Yustaga Province in 1623, as it was just to the east of Apalachee, but a severe shortage of friars by the late 1620s undoubtedly limited such contacts. In 1630 there were only twenty-seven friars to staff thirty-two doctrinas which, in turn, served over 200 villages, more than sixty of which had churches. In 1630 there were 20,000 baptized Indians and more than 50,000 natives who had been catechized but not baptized. Baptism was withheld because of the lack of friars to station among them to continue their instruction in the new faith and to ensure fidelity to their baptismal vows. It is likely that some of the more than 50,000 being catechized were Apalachee.

The formal move into Apalachee only three years later was likely in part a response to that situation. Prior contact with the Apalachee is known because the two friars who launched the mission effort in 1633 had a thorough knowledge of the Apalachee language.

THE BEGINNING OF FORMAL MISSIONS, 1633–1656

Pedro Muñoz and Francisco Martínez were the two friars entrusted with the Apalachee mission field. Governor Luis Horruytiner supported their efforts in the hope that conversion of Apalachee would solve St. Augustine's chronic food and labor shortages. Epidemics had already drastically reduced the population of the older mission provinces, and provisions were always in short supply. The governor hoped that Apalachee's ready access to the sea would facilitate the shipment of foodstuffs once a suitable port and channels to reach it were found.

Nothing is known of the circumstances that surrounded the two friars' arrival in Apalachee, and we have only conjecture about the villages in which they began to work. Indeed, with the exception of aspects of a 1647 revolt and the years 1655–1657, the first forty years of the Apalachee mission period are largely a great void. It is likely that the two head villages of Ivitachuco and Anhaica were among the first to receive the friars' attention, since it was standard practice and good policy to begin with leaders when they were amenable. Prieto's dealings with Ivitachuco in 1608 and the chief of Anhaica's trip to St. Augustine that same year also suggest that they would be early targets. Pedro Muñoz's presence at Ivitachuco at some time is indicated by one of its leading men having adopted the name Pedro Muñoz. Anhaica's early Christianization may be reflected in the choice of San Luis as the mission's Christian name, possibly in tribute to Governor Luis Horruytiner. The Ivitachuco chief's choice of Luis as his Christian name also could be a tribute to

The patron of San Luis is believed to be San Luis Rey de Francia (France's King St. Louis), whose feast day on August 25 became the principal festival of the Apalachee.

Friar baptizing Indian. Oil painting by and copyright of Gil Cohen. Reproduced courtesy of the artist and the U.S. Department of the Interior, National Park Service, San Antonio Missions National Historical Park.

the same governor and a possible marker for the time of his conversion. As late as 1639 there were still only two friars working in Apalachee. The first report on the progress of the conversions, made in 1635, claimed 5,000 baptisms out of a reputed population of 34,000. The governor reported over 1,000 baptisms in 1639, remarking that conversions were increasing more rapidly in Apalachee than anywhere else.

The only Apalachee mission of this early period whose founding date is known is San Damián de Cupaica. Its chief, described as the lord of over 200 vassals, journeyed to St. Augustine in 1639 to be baptized, with the governor as his godfather. After being christened Baltasar, the chief was then given a friar. The Cupaica mission appears to have been named for the incumbent governor Damián de Vega Castro y Pardo.

Establishment of the Apalachee missions followed the pattern of Florida's other hinterland missions, one that contrasts in a number of ways with that followed in New Mexico, Alta California, and Texas. The two friars began their work in Apalachee unaccompanied by soldiers and at the invitation of the native leaders, rather than imposing themselves on the population. There is no evidence for use of the reduction or *congregación* system to bring the natives to sites chosen by the

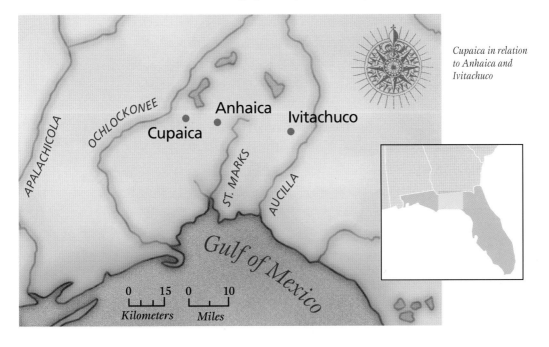

Cupaica in relation to Anhaica and Ivitachuco

friars. Florida's Franciscans established their missions in Apalachee where native villages already existed. When mission locations were changed, the moves were made at the behest of the natives or governors and were designed to satisfy the interests of one or the other, rather than those of the friars.

In contrast to the friars who established the first missions in New Mexico and California, Florida's friars did not bring large herds of cattle, horses, or sheep to strengthen their hand in convincing natives to accept their tutelage. If there was ultimately an overwhelming Spanish presence in Apalachee, it was represented in part by the governor in St. Augustine and his deputy or lieutenant at San Luis and, in the last quarter century of the mission era, in part by Spanish settlers and ranchers who increased the Hispanic population significantly. Many of these Spaniards were related by blood or marriage to an extended family whose members held the deputy governorship for most of that quarter century.

Although economic considerations were a factor motivating Florida's governors involved in the establishment of missions, none of Florida's missions is known to have become an economic enterprise dominated by friars. This was not the case at missions in other parts of the New World, such as those in California or the Jesuits' Tupi-Guarani missions of the Parana and Paraguay basins of South America. Neither *encomienda* (jurisdiction over an area and its inhabitants), tribute, nor enslavement of natives was a regular part of the Spanish regime in Florida. Encomienda was never introduced, and the several early attempts to introduce enslavement were quickly halted by the Crown. In general, a paid labor draft known as *repartimiento* was the only formal economically exploitative Spanish institution imposed on Florida's natives, and even it was resisted in Apalachee from 1608 to 1647. The labor draft was finally introduced in 1647 as the price for amnesty granted to most of the natives involved in a revolt that year against the Spaniards.

Tribute was introduced to a degree, in an informal sense. In Apalachee, as in other provinces in which soldiers were eventually stationed after the missions were established, natives were expected to contribute some of the food and the cacina or native tea that the soldiers consumed. Similarly, they were expected to carry soldiers' bedding from post to post without pay and perform other such chores interpreted as constituting service to the king.

The presence of soldiers in the province from the late 1630s and expansion of the mission effort in the early 1640s brought the first trouble. The first four or five soldiers arrived in Apalachee around 1638. They purchased supplies for the governors from the natives. They also served as his fiscal agents at the port at St. Marks, which was established to bring supplies for the friars and soldiers and to ship out native produce purchased for the support of St. Augustine.

It is not clear whether the soldiers had a common domicile during the first years they were stationed in Apalachee. They spent part of their time visiting some of the villages in the province. On those occasions they were lodged and fed in the village's principal council house as any other guest or traveler would have been.

Soldiers probably stayed in various council houses as they traveled from village to village throughout the province. Detail of oil painting "Military Muster at San Luis de Talimali, 1685" by John Briggs. A Florida National Guard Heritage painting. Reproduced courtesy of the Florida National Guard, St. Augustine, Florida. This work was commissioned and purchased in 1992 by the Florida National Guard as part of the Florida's Art in State Buildings Program (Florida Statute 255.043).

PRELUDE TO TROUBLE

The locations of the Amacano, Chacato, and Apalachicola in relation to the Apalachee

The soldiers' arrival probably stirred concern on the part of the Apalachee. Whereas Apalachee had for many years asked friars to come, there is no indication that they requested soldiers in the province. The inevitable liaisons that soldiers formed with Apalachee women were undoubtedly a source of friction and viewed by the friars as an obstacle to their work.

One of the soldiers was probably the governor's agent in negotiations that took place in 1639 and ended chronic warfare between the Apalachee and their neighbors to the west and north-northwest, the Amacano, Chacato, and Apalachicola. As desirable as peace might have seemed, the closing of this last outlet for the Apalachee's warrior spirit became a significant drawback for an important and influential segment of Apalachee society, the warrior caste. The existence of this caste was a major reason for chronic warfare. Becoming a renowned warrior was one of the principal ways of achieving status and, for ordinary Indian males, a principal source of upward mobility. The elimination of such opportunities doubtless angered many Apalachee men and their families.

The Spaniards' intention of fostering European settlement in the province and maintaining closer supervision over the native rulers was made clear when a newly arrived governor, Benito Ruíz de Salazar Vallecilla, appointed Claudio Luis de Florencia in mid-1645 as Apalachee's first deputy governor. Claudio Luis and his extended family resided in the village of San Luis de Inihaica, which was probably then in the general vicinity of the Anhaica of de Soto's time. He had been stationed earlier at St. Marks to collect customs duties. Governor Ruíz de Salazar himself visited Apalachee not long after his appointment of Florencia. During that trip he made arrangements for the establishment of a wheat and cattle ranch known as the Asile Hacienda in Yustaga Province on Apalachee's eastern border, but it eventually impinged on lands belonging to Apalachee as well.

The rapid expansion of the mission effort in the early 1640s and the consequent increase in the proportion of Apalachee who were Christianized probably awakened fears among the considerable number who remained non-Christians that they might eventually be pressured or forced to adopt the new ways. After the arrival of the soldiers and the deputy governor, it is likely that steps were taken to eliminate all vestiges of Apalachee's native cult, if that had not been done already under the influence of the paramount chief.

Apalachee Warrior Customs

As it was with the Apalachee's neighbors, the Apalachicola and Creek, the first step toward entry into the warrior caste was probably to be given a war name. Such a distinction could be achieved simply by being present at an encounter where an enemy scalp was taken. Among the Apalachee, a man who had taken one scalp achieved full warrior status and was known as tascaia. Advancement to higher rank, such as noroco, required the taking of additional scalps. The aspirant to the highest rank of nicoguadca had to kill seven recognized warriors or tascaias and three higher-ranked warriors.

Emboldened by the growing strength of the Christian element, some of the less tolerant and more puritanical friars began to forbid native dances that had associations with the native cult and deities or that the friars considered obscene. Some friars forbade playing the ball game in the villages under their jurisdiction. At times, Franciscans baptized Indian leaders who had multiple wives without making it sufficiently clear that as Christians they would be allowed only one wife. Friars and Spanish authorities also usually took the position that once an Indian accepted baptism, no backsliding or departure in any form from the new faith would be permitted. The friars also believed that coercive means should be used, if necessary, to compel such natives to live as Christians. These attitudes produced trouble.

The presence of the soldiers, the increase in the number of friars, and expansion of Spanish trading activities led to growing labor demands on the Indians. The governor's visit to Apalachee and to Indian provinces beyond Apalachee undoubtedly created a demand for porters, as did trading activities by soldiers in the governor's name. Establishment of the governor's Asile Hacienda also greatly increased demand for an Indian work force, in effect overruling the Apalachee leaders' refusal to contribute such labor.

The Apalachee Revolt of 1647

Growing concerns and grievances precipitated a serious revolt that began in February 1647. The native leaders who planned the revolt lured the Florencias away from San Luis—since its chief was not a party to the movement—by inviting the family to a fiesta at the mission of San Antonio de Bacuqua. The Apalachee killed three friars, as well as the deputy governor and his family members who were living with him: his wife and a married pregnant daughter along with her husband and child. The unborn child was cut from the mother's womb. The deputy governor also had a teen-aged daughter with him. She appears to have been particularly bold and was preaching the word of God to the Indians as the others were being tortured. In reprisal, the Apalachee cut off her breasts and her tongue. This level of violence indicates the intensity of the rebels' animosity toward the beginning of Spanish settlement in the region. Descendants of Claudio Luis were to dominate the Spanish community at San Luis in the last quarter of the century.

The soldiers escaped attack because they were at the governor's hacienda when the revolt began. Seven of the eight existing mission compounds were burned by the rebels, who included non-Christian Apalachee, many of the more recently

*Apalachee warriors
in revolt*

converted Apalachee, and visiting warriors belonging to the Chisca nation from a
settlement at the mouth of the Apalachicola River. Loyal Christian Apalachee
spirited the rest of the friars out of the province.

On learning of the revolt, authorities in St. Augustine hastily dispatched thirty-
one soldiers who recruited 500 Timucua warriors as allies as they headed westward.
Before these reinforcements could reach Apalachee, they were engaged by a much
larger rebel force in a day-long battle. The encounter was basically a standoff,

although the rebels were the first to retire from the field. Having exhausted their powder and shot, the Spaniards withdrew to St. Augustine believing that forces would have to be recruited from Cuba to regain control of the province. A smaller Spanish and Timucua force that was sent back to counter any further rebel forays

A study by Edward Jonas.
Reproduced courtesy of the artist.

into Timucua territory learned that the rebels were in disarray, disheartened by their losses and the unexpected rapidity of the Spanish response. Since it was planting time, the native rebels had not expected the Spaniards to be able to recruit many warriors in Timucua. They had also hoped that they would have time to consolidate their support among the Christian Apalachee and form alliances with other non-Christian provinces to prevent a reassertion of Spanish control in Apalachee.

This small Spanish and Timucua group, supported by loyal Christian Apalachee, were able to force or persuade the rebels to surrender and to hand over their leaders for trial. Twelve of the rebel leaders considered most responsible for the Spanish deaths were executed. Another twenty-six received terms of forced labor at the royal works in St. Augustine. The rest won a general pardon in exchange for the Apalachee rulers' promise to provide labor to the Spanish authorities, which they had resisted until then. The burned missions were quickly rebuilt by many of the same natives who had destroyed them, and over the ensuing twenty years or so all of the non-Christian Apalachee became Christians.

Apalachee Province after the Revolt

In 1651, shortly after the death of Governor Ruíz de Salazar who had established the Asile Hacienda, the ranch was dismantled at the request of the friars, the Apalachee chiefs, and the chief of Asile. The deceased governor's son had sold the hacienda and its accoutrements to the Crown, even though the land on which it was located was not his to sell. Friars also persuaded a new acting governor to remove the deputy governor and his soldiers from Apalachee, leaving the friars as the only Spaniards in the province.

Despite the removal of the main sources of conflict, Indian unrest reappeared in the mid-1650s under a new regular governor who assumed office in 1654. Epidemics had been taking a heavy toll on Indian and Spanish lives since 1650. There was growing dissatisfaction in Apalachee over the ongoing labor draft, probably because of a link made between those working in St. Augustine and those who succumbed to disease. The draft required each village to provide a specified number of men each year to travel to St. Augustine and work on Crown projects such as the wooden fort, or on farms belonging to Spanish soldiers who had families. Although the workers were to be paid a set minimum wage and meals, the travel and working conditions were harsh. The migrants were often required to carry cargo on their backs to St. Augustine and were frequently not allowed to return home when promised. They were often cheated by being paid in inferior or undesirable goods rather than in money or given an IOU when the government was short of funds or trade goods. When Apalachee leaders initially accepted the obligation, they were expecting it to last only a short time as punishment for the revolt.

Shortly after the new governor assumed office, he returned the deputy governor and two soldiers to Apalachee. He spoke of expanding the garrison and building a fort there and of reintroducing Spanish settlers to the province. He also criticized the abolition of the Asile Hacienda, which the Apalachee had championed.

Apalachee men were expected to assist in Spanish construction.

The Timucua Revolt of 1656

The unrest exploded into revolt in western Timucua early in 1656 when the governor, fearing an attack on St. Augustine by forces from Cromwell's England, ordered Indian warriors to come from the interior provinces to assist in the city's defense. He insisted that each warrior bring seventy-five pounds of corn on his back for his own sustenance. The Timucua leaders were angered—not by the call for warriors but by the governor's insistence that leaders and important warriors carry cargo. As "officers and gentlemen" they considered themselves exempt from such demeaning tasks. Despite other more important grievances, the insult implicit in that demand provided a good rallying point for revolt. Although the Timucua leaders sent a protest against being made to bear cargo, they decided to rebel before receiving the governor's reply.

The western Timucua warrior contingent gathered at Ivitachuco along with a force from Apalachee. They met with the governor's envoy but said nothing to him about their dissatisfaction. On the advice of Apalachee's deputy governor, Antonio de Sartucha, who apparently was based at Ivitachuco at the time, the Timucua contingent left first in the company of a soldier-interpreter named Esteban Solana, who had come with the governor's envoy. Sartucha advised keeping the two groups apart because they would steal from each other and cause trouble if they traveled together. Sending them at different times also would ease congestion at river crossings. The governor's envoy remained behind to accompany the Apalachee contingent. While he was waiting to set out, he sent one of Apalachee's two soldiers to Asile to pack some maize to bring along on their trip. That soldier and Solana became the revolt's first two victims. About two o'clock that afternoon, Asile's Fray Joseph Bamba galloped into Ivitachuco with the news that western Timucua had risen in revolt. Solana and the soldier from Apalachee had been killed after the province's head chief, the cacique of San Martín, ordered the warriors to kill any Spaniards (except friars) that they could find.

That development effectively isolated Sartucha, the governor's envoy, and the one remaining soldier stationed in Apalachee. Sartucha and the envoy's first move was to dismiss the assembled Apalachee warriors, telling them to return to their villages. Sartucha dispatched his one remaining soldier with two Apalachee Indians to bring news of the revolt to the governor. He instructed them to avoid the roads and to give the settled portion of Timucua a wide enough berth to evade capture. A major problem was the absence of Apalachee's paramount leader, the chief of Ivitachuco, who had gone to St. Augustine a little earlier with the province's labor-draft contingent.

To enlist the Apalachee in the struggle, the rebels spread rumors in the province that the governor had imprisoned Ivitachuco's chief and the workers with the intention of selling them as slaves. The rumors sparked such unrest that a majority of Apalachee's chiefs were allegedly ready to join the revolt. Eventually they were dissuaded by one of their more influential chiefs and possibly by a lingering resentment of the Timucua's role in thwarting the Apalachee revolt nine years earlier. The perception of danger was sufficient to prompt five of Apalachee's friars to leave on a ship sailing for Cuba. They perished en route when the vessel sank.

Before the governor could reply to Sartucha's note, he learned of the unrest caused by the rumors of the imprisonment of Ivitachuco's chief when Apalachee's leaders sent several Indians to St. Augustine to investigate the matter. The governor prevailed on Apalachee's paramount chief to send his heir and several of his leading men to assure the Apalachee that the rumors were untrue and to tell them to remain calm. They accompanied Apalachee's lone soldier and three other soldiers who carried the governor's reply to Sartucha. The governor, who was fearful of English attack at the time of the revolt, did not send aid for three or four months until the threat of attack had abated because of the stormy seas that mark the fall season along Florida's Atlantic coast.

Spanish forces finally arrived in Apalachee in September 1656. As many as 500 Apalachee warriors accompanied them when they moved against the palisade the rebels had built near Machava in Yustaga Province. The Apalachee assisted the Spaniards in detaining rebel leaders who agreed to meet with the Spanish commander at the Machava council house. The rest of the rebels disbanded peacefully after learning of the detention of most of their leaders. On receiving this news, Governor Diego de Rebolledo set out for Ivitachuco on November 27, where the captives were being held to await sentencing. Governor Rebolledo held the trials during December.

Beginning in January 1657, the governor conducted a formal visitation of Apalachee Province, going from mission to mission to hear any complaints that the Indians might have had against the resident Spaniards. Since there were rumors of a possible revolt among the Apalachee, he sought to appease them by listening to their complaints. The criticisms elicited were directed almost exclusively at the friars, while the soldiers were portrayed positively, so it is likely that, in reality, Rebolledo made it clear that he would hear only complaints against the friars. In response, the governor addressed some of the Apalachee's concerns: he told the friars not to prohibit the Indians' ball games and dances and not to require Indians to carry cargo for them, and he forbade punishing Indian leaders for their infractions against Christian morals. Although the governor increased Apalachee's garrison to twelve men, he postponed his plans for further enlargement of the garrison and for building a genuine fort. He also deferred his plans to establish a civilian Spanish settlement in the province.

DISTRIBUTION OF THE APALACHEE MISSIONS IN THE MID-SEVENTEENTH CENTURY

The record of Governor Rebolledo's 1657 visitation provides the earliest and most detailed look at the missions and other villages of Apalachee Province. It identifies the chiefs of principal villages and the satellite settlements under their jurisdiction that had their own chiefs. Occasionally other leading men are named as well. The record also identifies twenty-four satellite settlements, specifying the head chiefs to whom they were subordinate. The list of subordinate villages is not complete because a chief or another of the settlement's leaders had to attend the visitation at the mission center in order for the village to be mentioned. Six additional subordinate villages were identified in later documents.

The importance of Ivitachuco and San Luis is indicated by the number of leaders mentioned in addition to their head chief and by their many satellite settlements. Later documents reveal that San Luis had two satellite settlements in addition to the ones mentioned. The visitation record identified Don Luis de Ibitachucu as the most important Apalachee chief. He was the only chief present who was literate, although the native militia captains at Ivitachuco and San Luis

List from the 1657 Visitation Record

I.   San Damián de Cupaica—Baltasar, principal chief
      1. Nicapana—Bentura, chief
      2. Faltassa—Martín, chief
      3. San Cosme—Bentura, chief
      4. San Lucas—chief

II.   Santa María de Bacucua—Alonso, principal chief
      1. Guaça—Martín, chief

III. San Pedro de Patali—Baltasar, principal chief
      1. Ajamano—Francisco, chief
      2. Talpahique—Alonso, chief

IV.   San Luis de Inihaica—Francisco Luis, principal chief
      Antonio García, its captain and cousin of the chief
      Antonio de Ynija—a leading man
      Pedro García—a leading man
      1. Abaslaco—Gerónimo, chief
      2. San Francisco—Francisco, chief

V.   San Juan de Aspalaga—Alonso, principal chief
      1. Pansacola—Manuel, chief
      2. Sabe—Christóbal, chief
      3. Jipe—Santiago, heir to the chieftainship

VI.   San Martín de Thomole—Antonio, the inija, representing the absent principal chief
      1. Ciban—Bernardo, chief
      2. San Diego—Diego, Chief
      3. Samoche—Bernardo, chief

VII. San Joseph de Ocuya—Benito Ruiz, principal chief
      1. Sabacola—Gaspar, chief
      2. Ajapaxca—Santiago, chief
      3. Chali—Jerónimo, chief

VIII. San Francisco de Ocone—Francisco Martín, principal chief
      1. San Miguel—Alonso Martín, chief

IX.   Santa María de Ayubale—Martín, principal chief
      Alonso, a leading man and brother of the chief
      1. Cutachuba—Adrián, a leading man

X.   San Lorenzo de Ibitachuco—Don Luis de Ibitachucu, principal chief
      Lorenzo Moreno, captain of the place
      Francisco and Santiago, leading men
      1. San Juan—Andrés, chief and uncle of Don Luis
      2. San Pablo—Pedro Muñoz, chief
      3. San Nicolás—Thomás, chief
      4. Ajapasca—Fabián, chief

XI.   San Miguel de Azile—Gaspar, principal chief and uncle of Ybitachuco's Don Luis
      Lucas, identified as chief, but no village mentioned
      Juan de Medina, principal heir to Lucas
      Lázaro, a leading man and father of the chief of Sabe

This list is drawn from the 1657 visitation record and reflects the order in which Governor Rebolledo held the visitation of the various missions.

were sufficiently literate to sign their names to the visitation record. Don Luis de Ibitachucu was also the only one dignified with the title Don in the visitation record. Later in the century all principal chiefs mentioned were given the title. The four satellite settlements of Cupaica also reliably reflect its importance. It was the most populous of Apalachee's missions in 1689. Asile, the eleventh village noted,

was Timucua rather than Apalachee, but Rebolledo identified it as part of Apalachee as did one of the de Soto chroniclers. The accession of an Apalachee as its chief was recent and may have been a consequence of the 1656 revolt. In 1651 its chief was a Timucua named Manuel, who generally is credited with writing one of the two extant letters in the Timucua language, although another source indicates that he was not literate. In addition to the settlements listed that had chiefs, other Apalachee lived in small hamlets of three to five houses or on isolated farmsteads scattered through the countryside.

Comparison of the 1657 record with a 1655 listing of the missions that gives their distance from St. Augustine indicates that in 1657 only Ivitachuco, Ayubale, and Ocone were located in the eastern half of the province. By 1675, however, Ocuya and Aspalaga had become part of the eastern constellation of Apalachee missions, providing more of a balance between the two halves of the province. Nothing is known about the reason for such moves. Comparison

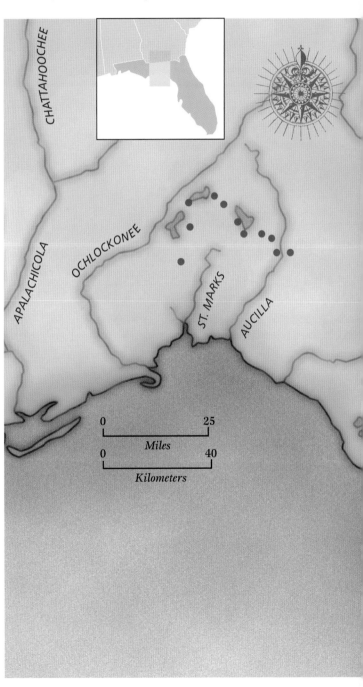

Distribution of Apalachee missions in the mid-seventeenth century

of San Luis's location vis-à-vis Cupaica in 1655 and in 1675, when distances between individual missions were given, suggests that when San Luis was relocated in 1656, it moved one league (about two and one-half miles) westward, assuming that Cupaica occupied the same site in 1675 that it did in 1655.

By 1672, an eleventh mission, known variously as Santa Cruz de Capoli and Santa Cruz de Ychutafun (meaning Deertown), had been established on a hill on the western edge of the St. Marks River lowlands. It probably was founded by Spanish order to serve as a way station on the royal road heading east toward St. Augustine. The new mission would have lessened the traveling distance between the last of the western missions and the first of those in the east. The moving of Aspalaga may have been similarly motivated. There are indications that Ocuya was toward the north, off the regular route.

ARCHAEOLOGICAL EVIDENCE OF THE EARLIEST MISSIONS

There are few archaeological data associated with the first missionary and military forays into Apalachee Province because of the highly mobile nature of these first Spanish emissaries and the ephemeral signs typically left on any landscape by a few individuals. Even the 1539–1540 assemblage associated with the de Soto entourage at Anhaica is small and fragmentary, despite the fact that it represents the accumulated debris of hundreds of men who lived at the site for five months and who received additional provisions during their stay from ships moored in Tampa Bay.

The first Spaniards to reside in Apalachee probably moved from village to village where they stayed in community lodges and depended on the native population for

Conjectural view of the west end of the church at San Luis

Location of Apalachee missions that have been
archaeologically tested and tentatively identified

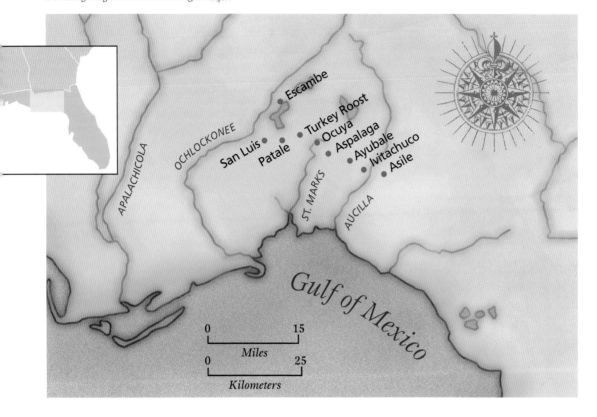

many of their supplies. It is therefore not surprising that many of the early villages that housed friars and soldiers would not be distinguishable archaeologically from other Apalachee villages. Even the recovery of some European materials could be evidence of gift giving or trade rather than of an actual Spanish presence.

After the construction of churches in Christianized Apalachee villages, the archaeological record plays a greater role in identifying mission sites. However, because most of the Apalachee missions consisted of a church and cemetery in an otherwise pristine Indian village, it is still difficult to determine the identifications of respective missions.

In the 1970s and 1980s, B. Calvin Jones of the Florida Bureau of Archaeological Research conducted limited testing on numerous possible mission sites in Apalachee Province. His work

Artifacts recovered by Henry Baker at La Chua Hacienda included nail fragments, a strap hinge, and daub.

resulted in the tentative identification of a number of missions, most of which contained mission-period artifacts, European architectural remains, and Christian-style burials. These preliminary identifications were based primarily on reckoning from the only known mission location at the time, San Luis de Talimali, using the approximate distances recorded in the documents. Only one mission besides San Luis has been thoroughly investigated archaeologically. San Pedro y San Pablo de Patale was first excavated by Jones and, subsequently, by Rochelle A. Marrinan. More than a decade of fieldwork has resulted in the identification of a number of structures at Patale including a religious complex, a possible dwelling, and a pre-mission council house.

The village of Ivitachuco and Asile Hacienda are two sites for which there should be ample archaeological evidence for firm identifications. Ivitachuco was a principal village and home to Deputy Governor Sartucha in the mid-1600s. The site should have a major public building complex that includes a large plaza and council house, a church, and possibly some type of European-style residence. A bell tower is recorded as having been added late in the century. Significant amounts of Spanish materials, particularly domestic and military artifacts, would also be expected.

Similarly, the identification of the Asile Hacienda should be easily confirmed through the remains of Spanish buildings and the recovery of ranching implements. A complete auction inventory provides clear descriptions of the buildings associated with the hacienda and the types of tools and equipment used on the ranch (see chapter 3). Although the items listed in the inventory were sold when the ranch was dismantled, remains of similar equipment that was lost or broken when the farm was active should be evident.

Among the various types of hardware found at La Chua Hacienda were tacks, nails, and spikes.

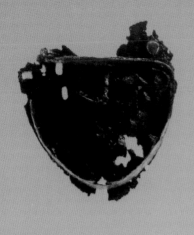

These artifacts from La Chua Hacienda
near Gainesville are similar to those that
would be expected from other Spanish
ranches in La Florida, including Asile
Hacienda.

Top: *padlock box and spur rowel*
Middle: *sword cross guard*
Bottom: *flintlock mechanism*

0 1 2 3 4 5 6 7 8 9 10

Centimeters

ESTABLISHMENT OF THE CAPITAL AT MISSION SAN LUIS

At some point during 1656, the deputy governor and his soldiers established their headquarters at the site presently identified with Mission San Luis de Talimali. Sartucha also prevailed upon the chief of San Luis to move to the new site with his people. Prior to the move, the San Luis mission was located to the east of the new site, probably on or near Anhaica, which de Soto commandeered for his winter camp. In other words, the corporate entity that became Mission San Luis was a lineal descendant of the one known to de Soto. From 1656 until the Spanish and Apalachee abandoned the province in mid-1704, Mission San Luis functioned as the western headquarters or capital of the Florida hinterland, where the people acknowledged the sovereignty of Spain's king.

Nothing is known of the details of that move except that San Luis's chief agreed to move his village to the site in order to be near the Spaniards, and he promised to build the deputy governor and his soldiers a capacious blockhouse. However, by the spring of 1657, the chief was objecting to Rebolledo's plan to expand the garrison to twelve men. The chief suggested that six soldiers and a squad leader would be enough. He swas concerned with a shortage of food, the

disruption associated with the recent moving of his village, and unspecified difficulties that occurred during the previous winter. In part, he was probably bowing to pressure from the other Apalachee chiefs and the friars who were waging a campaign for the withdrawal of all the soldiers. Adrián de Canizares y Osorio, who had led the Spanish forces sent by the governor to Ivitachuco in September 1656, was installed as Apalachee's deputy governor during Governor Rebolledo's stay in the province.

CHAPTER 3

The Mission Community at San Luis

Mission San Luis served as the western capital of Spanish Florida for nearly a half century, from 1656 to 1704. With more than 1500 Apalachee and Spanish residents, San Luis was one of the most densely populated of the mission towns. It was a principal village of the Apalachee Indians and home to some of their most powerful leaders. By the 1670s, San Luis was also home to a permanent Spanish deputy governor, a garrison, friars, and civilians and their extended families. In this respect, San Luis was more similar to St. Augustine than other missions were. Rather than having just a single friar living in an otherwise native village, San Luis had a cross-section of Spanish residents living with the Apalachee in a truly multicultural community.

Conjectural view of San Luis by Edward Jonas prior to archaeological investigations at the site

THE SPANISH RESIDENTS

Apalachee's First Family

The appointment of Juan Fernández de Florencia as deputy governor may have been an unpleasant surprise for many among the Apalachee. He was a son of the first deputy governor, Claudio Luis de Florencia, who was killed by the Apalachee in 1647. The records do not indicate whether Fernández de Florencia harbored ill feelings over their killing of his father, mother, and other members of his family almost thirty years earlier. A new governor, Pablo de Hita Salazar, commissioned Fernández de Florencia to reinstitute the plans for a Spanish settlement in the province, plans that had been postponed indefinitely after the killing of Claudio Luis in 1647 and the Crown's abrupt removal of Governor Rebolledo in 1658. Upon the outbreak of trouble among the recently missionized Chacato in mid-1675, Hita Salazar expressed concern that many Apalachee were acquiring firearms and munitions from ships at St. Marks. He suggested to the Crown that it was time to go forward with Governor Rebolledo's plans of a generation earlier to build a genuine fort in the province. He saw the Chacato troubles as a good pretext for the Spanish authorities to build the fort and to thwart Apalachee opposition to the plan.

As Fernández de Florencia launched Spanish settlement and ranching in the province, his nephews and nieces figured prominently as members of the province's Spanish rancher elite and landed nobility. He turned Apalachee into somewhat of a Florencia fiefdom in the course of the last quarter of the seventeenth century. Juan Fernández himself set the pattern. He was the deputy governor into the early 1680s and remained in Apalachee to establish a ranch after his term ended. His successor as deputy governor, Andrés Péres, had been his second-in-command and was married to a Catalina de Florencia. The rest of the Apalachee Florencias were Juan Fernández's brother, Pedro de Florencia, Pedro's wife, and a host of their children (see appendix).

Pedro, like his brother Juan Fernández, had been in Apalachee prior to 1675. Both were familiar with the language. When Governor Hita Salazar learned of the

Artist's conception of the Spanish village at San Luis

Chacato trouble, he dispatched Pedro with a few soldiers to assist his brother Juan Fernández in dealing with the crisis and to assess the situation for the governor. Hita Salazar described Pedro as having had experience in the province and as being an interpreter of the Apalachee language. Juan Fernández also was interested enough in the customs and legends of the Apalachee to have had a copy made of Fray Juan de Paiva's Apalachee ball game manuscript with the intention of sending it to his brother Francisco, a Jesuit priest working in Mexico. It was Juan Fernández's copy of the manuscript that was preserved when the visitor, Domingo de Leturiondo, commandeered it in 1677 in order to put it into the record of his visitation.

The two most prominent of Pedro's children who established themselves at San Luis were his first-born, Juana Cathalina de Florencia, and his third child, Diego de Florencia. Juana Cathalina married Jacinto Roque Pérez in 1675 at the tender age of thirteen. Beginning in the 1680s, Captain Roque Pérez would be deputy governor of Apalachee three times before the end of the century. In the 1690s, he built the new San Luis blockhouse and became one of the province's most important ranchers with property in Apalachee worth an estimated 10,000 pesos in 1704. Juana Cathalina became infamous for her mistreatment of various Apalachee and her demands for unpaid labor from them. The couple appear to have become permanent residents of Apalachee around 1678 when their first child, Pedro Gregorio, was baptized in St. Augustine. They had ten living children by 1704. As Pedro Gregorio was the only one of them baptized in St. Augustine, the other nine must have been born and baptized at San Luis.

Artist's conception of Juana Cathalina

Only a few Spanish women lived at San Luis, most of whom probably had Apalachee servants. Juana Cathalina was married to the deputy governor and they had ten children. She was a bad-tempered woman who once slapped a leader in the face for not bringing her fish. Her actions were typical of the attitude of many Spaniards toward the Apalachee.

Artist's conception of Diego de Florencia

Diego de Florencia was one of the wealthiest traders at San Luis. He owned several ships which transported hides, beef, corn, tallow, lard, hams, and chickens to Havana in exchange for goods coming in from the Orient, Europe, and other parts of the New World.

Diego de Florencia was a rancher, ship owner, occasional treasure salvor, and one of the most active participants in the trade between Apalachee and Havana. Although Diego was only ten years old in 1677, he was listed at that time as owner of record of a frigate named *The Nativity of St. Francis of Padua*, which pirates captured in the port of St. Marks. Diego was living in Havana at the time, probably attending school even though he already held the rank of ensign. Captain Juan de la Rosa was in charge of Diego's captured ship as its administrator. In addition to the documentation describing the capture of Rosa's ship, Rosa's presence on the St. Marks River was attested to archaeologically some years ago when divers found a pot bearing his name. In 1699, Diego was mentioned as living at the house of Juan Fernández de Florencia, along with Diego's brother Francisco.

Francisco and two other siblings became residents of Apalachee Province as adults and probably spent time there as children. Claudio, Pedro's second-born, became a Franciscan friar and served as San Luis's pastor in 1703. Francisco, Pedro's fifth child, became a rancher late in the century after being banished to Apalachee for his violent and disorderly behavior in St. Augustine. His conduct did not improve during his stay in Apalachee. While he and forty Chacato Indians were hunting buffalo in west Florida, they killed sixteen of twenty-four Tasquique Indians who were coming peaceably to San Luis to trade. Because Francisco's brother-in-law, Jacinto Roque Pérez, was the deputy governor and chief magistrate, no action was taken against Francisco and his Indian cohorts despite complaints by Apalachee's paramount chief, don Patricio Hinachuba. Don Patricio warned that if the murderers were not punished, the murdered Indians' fellow villagers and allies would inevitably retaliate against the province.

María Magdalena de Florencia was baptized in 1675, the last of Pedro's children whose baptism is recorded in St. Augustine's parish records. She eventually married another Apalachee rancher, a soldier named Diego Jiménez. They had five living children by 1704.

It is probable that Pedro and his wife, Francisca de Urisa, moved to Apalachee some time after the birth of María Magdalena. Francisca de Urisa's presence in the province is recorded for the mid-1680s. María Magdalena's marriage to Jiménez probably occurred in Apalachee; the marriage was not recorded in St. Augustine. And when her brother Francisco married Ana María Argüelles in St. Augustine in July 1697, Pedro and Francisca's place of origin was given as Apalachee.

Other factors buttressed the Florencia clan's power and impunity in the province. Francisco Romo de Urisa, a relative of Pedro's wife, served a term as deputy governor during this period. The royal treasurer, Joaquín de Florencia, who represented another branch of the family, served as the governor's official visitor to the province in 1694–1695. Juan de Ayala Escobar, who was related to the family by marriage, conducted two subsequent visitations. Indeed, the Florencias had

blood and marriage ties with a number of influential families in St. Augustine, including the Argüelleses, Menéndez Márquezes, Horruytiners, Canizareses, and Mejías. Among Apalachee's leading ranchers, only Marcos Delgado of the Hacienda Our Lady of the Rosary and Joseph Salinas of the Hacienda of San Joseph de Upalucha are not known to have had close ties to the Florencias.

Domingo de Leturiondo deserves mention as well because of his extensive experience in the province beginning at least as early as the 1660s. He served three times as Apalachee's deputy governor and conducted visitations of the province in the governor's name in 1672, 1677, and 1685. He was appointed Protector of the Indians in the 1680s and directed the first abortive inquiry into the Apalachee leaders' complaints against their deputy governor, Antonio Matheos. His son Alonso de Leturiondo, who served as St. Augustine's pastor for much of the 1680s and part of the 1690s, shared his father's interest in and concern for the province and the welfare of its natives.

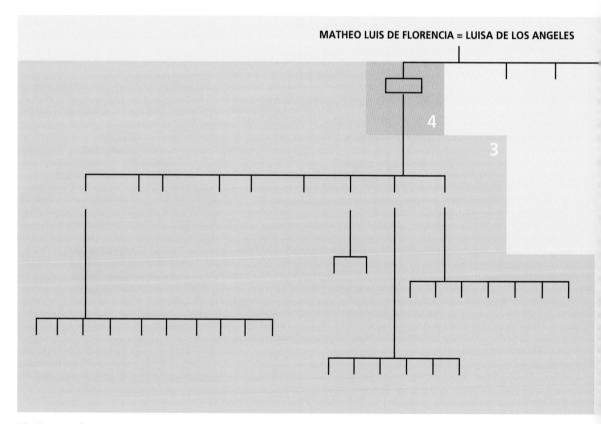

MATHEO LUIS DE FLORENCIA = LUISA DE LOS ANGELES

The Florencias (see appendix for full genealogy) exerted considerable political, military, and religious influence over Apalachee Province throughout the mission period.

THE FLORENCIA FAMILY OF SPANISH FLORIDA COLOR KEY

Color 1 & 3 – Descendants of MATHEO LUIS DE FLORENCIA and LUISA DE LOS ANGELES
Color 2 – Descendants of GASPAR FERNANDEZ PERETE and FRANCISCA DE LEIVA Y ARTEAGA
Color 3 – Descendants of PATRICIO and MARIANA DE LA ROCHA Y MENDOZA
Color 4 – Union of PATRICIO and MARIANA DE LA ROCHA Y MENDOZA
Color 5 – Union of MATEO LUIS and FRANCISCA LEIVA Y ARTEAGA
Color 6 – Union of CLAUDIO and JUANA DE LEIVA Y ARTEAGA

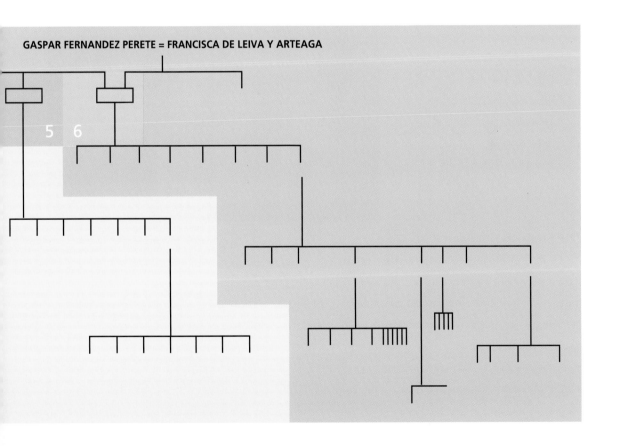

GASPAR FERNANDEZ PERETE = FRANCISCA DE LEIVA Y ARTEAGA

The San Luis Garrison in 1675

Captain Juan Fernández de Florencia, deputy governor

Adjutant Andrés Péres, second-in-command

Ensign Esteban de Luz

Ensign Joseph de Salinas

Juan López de Duenos

Elgo (?) de la Motta

Alonso García

Nicolás Días

Juan de Sandobal

Christóbal Fernández

Joseph Tinoco

Francisco Ruyz

Juan García

Alonso de Morales

Pedro de Torres

Juan Rodríguez

Manuel de Orta

Juan Antonio

Miguel de Ribas

Detail of oil painting by John Briggs. Reproduced courtesy of the Florida National Guard, St. Augustine, Florida.

The Spanish Garrison

From 1657 into the 1670s the garrison at San Luis seems to have fluctuated in size between twelve and twenty-five. An exception occurred in the early 1660s when the garrison may have grown to as many as forty. That large expansion was a momentary one linked to an exploratory expedition sent from San Luis toward the Choctaw country. The garrison consisted of only twelve men in mid-1668, and a governor gave its size as twenty-five men in October 1671. However, just over a year later it numbered only nineteen men, a level maintained apparently until at least 1675. For that year we have the names of the nineteen soldiers stationed at San Luis and at Apalachee's port of St. Marks. Of those, only Ensign Joseph de Salinas and

Pedro de Torres, in addition to Fernández de Florencia and Péres, are known to have been long-term residents of the province. Torres and Salinas were still there in 1695.

Spanish ships that visited the port of St. Marks frequently brought additional temporary Spanish residents of Apalachee, but it is not known how often they left the port to visit San Luis or other mission settlements. When the garrison list from 1675 was composed, his majesty's frigate *The Most Holy Trinity* was in port seeking provisions. It had a crew of twenty, who were identified by name and occupation. Five of them were soldiers.

The appearance of English traders from Charles Town in Apalachicola villages on the Chattahoochee River prompted an increase in the garrison to about forty during the 1680s, where its size stabilized more or less until 1704. However, that number was temporarily larger at times for the staffing of special military or exploratory expeditions. During Carolina Governor James Moore's 1702 siege of St. Augustine's castillo, almost ninety men capable of bearing arms from the Spanish community in Apalachee went to their aid, and an additional ten men from Pensacola joined the relief force. Undoubtedly some men remained in Apalachee to guard the blockhouse.

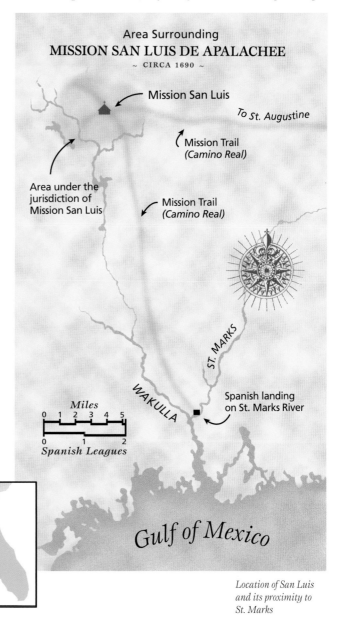

Location of San Luis and its proximity to St. Marks

THE APALACHEE RESIDENTS

Native Leaders at San Luis

Among Apalachee's native leaders during this period, a number of names appear frequently in connection with San Luis and the rest of the province, while others are mentioned only rarely or in passing. San Luis had a shadowy hereditary chief named Francisco Luis, first mentioned in 1675. His name recurs for the next fifteen years or so. Although he was referred to as the principal chief, he did not exercise his authority as such. The task of governing San Luis during that time fell

instead to a man named don Matheo Chuba, who held the title of native "governor." Since one of the meanings of *chuba* is "big," his name might be rendered in English colloquially as "Big Matt" or "Big Matthew." We are indebted to Matheo Chuba for one of the few references to Francisco Luis as legitimate chief of the village. In telling of an occasion in the

mid-1680s when Apalachee's deputy governor, Antonio Matheos, placed Matheo Chuba and his inija in irons, a soldier reported that the Indians of San Luis went to consult with the pair as "their heads and governors to ask what they should do." Rapport between Matheo Chuba and his friar at San Luis is reflected in Jacinto Roque Pérez's account of Chuba's reaction to this imprisonment when some of San Luis's people visited the imprisoned Chuba and the inija Bip Bentura to ask what the people of San Luis should do about it. Chuba replied that they should consult their priest and do what he ordered them to do. Concerned by the evident agitation of the Indians, Roque Pérez, along with his wife, Juana Cathalina, and her mother, appealed successfully to Matheos to release the two Indians. Matheo Chuba himself, in testifying on the same occasion, identified Francisco Luis as "principal cacique" and styled himself "governor of that place."

We do not know the reasons for the sidelining of Chief Francisco Luis during this extended period or for the installation of Matheo Chuba as "governor" to run the village in his place. It is possible that age was the reason if the Francisco Luis of the 1680s was the same Francisco Luis who was identified as principal chief of

*Chief (**background**) and inija (**foreground**)*
during council house ceremony

San Luis a generation earlier during the 1657 visitation. But Chief Francisco Luis was fit enough in the mid-1680s to consider making a trip to St. Augustine to deliver a complaint to the governor against the deputy governor, Antonio Matheos. On the other hand, Francisco Luis was not among the village's leaders who participated in a 1677 attack on a Chisca village.

The title "governor" was given commonly to a native in Spanish Florida who was the nephew-or niece-heir to the chieftainship in question, a person who had taken over the running of the village from the ruling aunt or uncle. This usually occurred when the old leader had become incapacitated by age or illness and when the successor did not want to assume the chieftainship formally out of respect for his still-living predecessor. Although Matheo Chuba's enjoyment of the title "don" suggests that he belonged to a chiefly line, there is no indication that Chuba was Francisco Luis's heir. And Chuba did not succeed to the San Luis chieftainship. Chuba was still alive in 1695 when a man named Usunaca Andrés was identified clearly as principal chief at San Luis. For some reason Usunaca Andrés was additionally given the title of "governor" that year during the visitation of the province.

Matheo Chuba's name first appeared in the report by "the principal leaders who went to make war on the Chiscas." The principal leaders were identified as "Juan Mendoza, Matheo Chuba, Bernardo, the cacique of Cupaica, and Bentura, the inija of San Luis" in that order. Placement of Mendoza's name first might be interpreted as meaning that he was then the most important of San Luis's leaders. But there is no indication that he ever held any position more important than that of parish interpreter at San Luis along with the rank of captain of San Luis. Matheo Chuba held the rank of fieldmaster. Chuba's importance even then is indicated by his having led the main body of the Apalachee force in the attack on the Chisca village, assisted by two unnamed captains, while Captains Bernardo and Mendoza (mentioned in that order) led the attacks on the east and west flanks, respectively.

Matheo Chuba achieved his greatest notoriety in the mid-1680s in conjunction with his inija Bip Bentura because they were frequently targets of the anger of Antonio Matheos. Chuba and Bentura appear to have been highly critical of Matheos and repeatedly requested that the governor remove him from office. In addition to jailing the two village leaders briefly, Matheos taunted Chuba for his close ties to the friars. On one occasion Matheos injured Bentura, striking him on

Artist's conception of Bip Bentura

As inija, or town manager, Bip Bentura was responsible for overseeing the preparation of the black drink. He was also in charge of native sentries and supervised the planting of the San Luis fields.

the head with a walnut club. In the 1688 letter written in the Apalachee language, "Don Matheo Chuba" appears first among the signatures of the leaders who were able to sign the letter.

Juan Mendoza is known best as the coauthor with Diego Salvador of the notebook on the origin myths and ceremonies associated with the ball game that Fray Paiva used in composing the ball game manuscript. Like Matheo Chuba, Mendoza was taunted by Antonio Matheos for his close ties with the friars. Matheos also deprived him of the right to have parish Indians cultivate his fields even though it was a customary privilege of parish interpreters.

Diego Salvador was the person who actually composed the notebook and wrote down the information using the Apalachee and Timucua languages. He was a Timucua from the province of Diminiyuti or Acuera, but he had come to Apalachee as a youth. His name first appeared in the 1657 visitation record as interpreter for both the Apalachee and Timucua speakers. He held the rank of sergeant major and served as royal interpreter in the service of the deputy governor at San Luis. His name last appeared in the 1677 visitation record, for which he served as interpreter for the visitation of the Apalachee missions.

COMMUNITY ORGANIZATION AT MISSION SAN LUIS

There is no evidence that the hilltop selected by the Spaniards for their headquarters in 1656 was ever occupied for any length of time prior to the mission settlement. Although a broad range of artifacts dating back to the Paleoindian period (at least 10,000 years ago) have been recovered at the site, they are isolated finds. The site was probably used only intermittently by passersby or for brief encampments in pre-mission times. Such a finding is remarkable in light of the fact that the prehistoric Apalachee favored elevated locations such as the Lake Jackson Mounds and the "Capitol Hill" complex of Anhaica for their premier villages, and San Luis is located atop one of Tallahassee's highest ridgetops at 208 feet above sea level. It is also a desirable location because of the ravine that cuts across the eastern edge of the hill in which seep springs run year round.

This Suwannee projectile point is one of the few Paleoindian artifacts ever found at San Luis.

The Spaniards no doubt appreciated the defensive advantages of the location when they selected it for their headquarters. To date, there has been no cartographic or documentary evidence found that illuminates the town plan of San Luis or any indication of which buildings were constructed first. Presumably, the deputy governor and his garrison would have deemed some type of temporary shelter of utmost importance while they waited for more permanent quarters to be built. Structural evidence pre-dating the construction of the major fort complex of the 1690s suggests that at least one blockhouse, or *casa fuerte*, may have been built in approximately the same area. This location would have afforded sentries a commanding view of the surrounding countryside, particularly to the north where invading forces generally originated.

The Plaza

It is presumed that the location of the central plaza must have been established at an early date and that the construction of the public buildings on the plaza followed soon after. The plaza at San Luis is something of an enigma. At 410 feet in diameter, its circular shape is atypical of most other Spanish colonial plazas that were rectangular or square. It is believed that the shape derives from Apalachee town planning traditions, but plazas have not been clearly identified archaeologically at other villages in Apalachee Province.

For Spaniards, large open plazas served as the center of community life where people met and open-air markets were held. It was also an ideal location for such activities as military drills and church processions. The plaza at Mission San Luis may have had a series of large crosses around its perimeter, as was the case at other

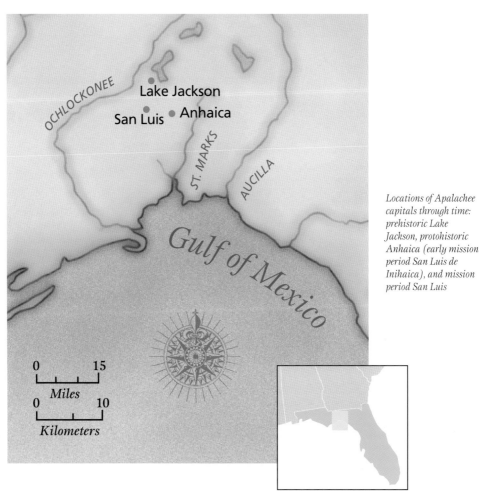

Locations of Apalachee capitals through time: prehistoric Lake Jackson, protohistoric Anhaica (early mission period San Luis de Inihaica), and mission period San Luis

Conceptual view of the southeastern edge of the plaza on market day.

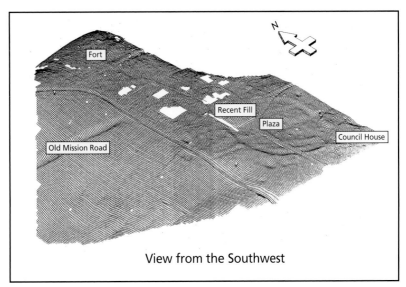

Features revealed through topographic mapping at two-meter intervals at San Luis

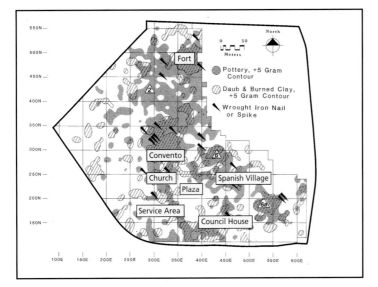

Distribution of archaeological remains at San Luis based on auger testing at ten-meter intervals across the site

Apalachee missions. Representing the fourteen stations of the cross, these symbolized the successive incidents from the Passion of Christ.

Among the Apalachee, the plaza was also the location for various social activities. However, its most important function was as the playing field for their traditional games, especially the one known as the ball game. The Apalachee ball game involved a single goal post which was raised in the center of the plaza.

The location of the plaza at San Luis was initially identified by a low earthen ridge revealed by topographic mapping. Documents indicate that the plaza was swept every day, suggesting that the town center was kept fairly clean of trash. Archaeology has confirmed that the area inside the plaza contains few artifacts, while the ridge itself contains an assortment of accumulated mission-period debris.

Two large public buildings faced onto the plaza at San Luis, the Apalachee council house and the Franciscan church. In pre-Christian times, the villages' main religious structure or temple probably stood at the opposite end of the plaza from the council house. This temple housed the Apalachee's gods, which personified forces of nature such as thunder and rain and heavenly bodies such as the sun and moon. The temple was replaced during the mission period by a Catholic church and friary. The Apalachee council house and the church at San Luis were situated directly across from one another on the southeast and northwest edges of the plaza, respectively.

Two houses have also been found near the perimeter of the central plaza, one an Apalachee dwelling and the other a Spanish residence. In both Apalachee and

Artist's rendering of the central plaza and archaeologically investigated buildings around its perimeter

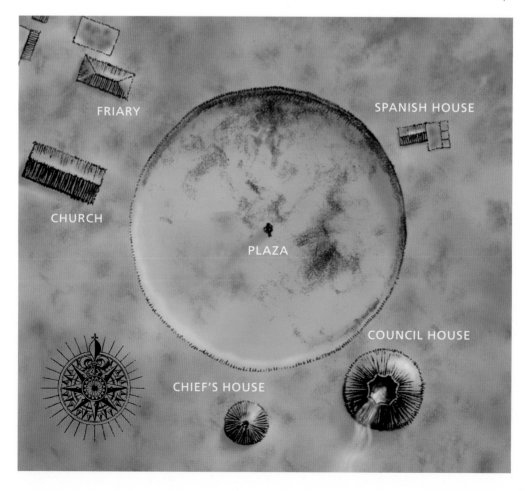

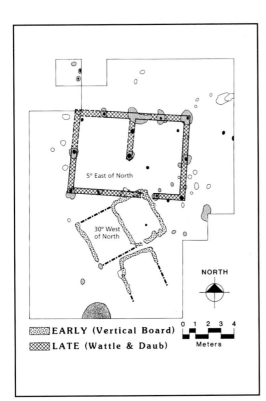

5° East of North

30° West
of North

NORTH

0 1 2 3 4
Meters

▨▨▨ EARLY (Vertical Board)
▨▨▨ LATE (Wattle & Daub)

The archaeological remains of these two overlapping house foundations provide evidence that houses in the Spanish village changed orientation through time.

Spanish settlements, living in such a prominent location was reserved for only the most important members of the community.

In virtually every respect, the layout of San Luis fails to comply with the royal ordinances of 1573 mandating the arrangement of New World towns. According to this Roman-derived plan, New World colonial communities were to be laid out on a grid starting with the establishment of a rectangular or square central plaza. Main thoroughfares were to radiate off of the main plaza in the four cardinal directions, thereby creating the appearance of a highly organized and civilized town. There is no evidence that this concept was taken into account during the planning of San Luis. The immense plaza is circular in shape, and none of the buildings across the site are oriented parallel or perpendicular to another, with the exception of the church and the friary; they are adjacent and roughly parallel to each other. Perhaps the strongest evidence that San Luis was not laid out on a grid is the variability of house orientation in the Hispanic residential area. The three dwellings identified archaeologically thus far in the Spanish village are oriented 30° west of north, 5° east of north, and 156° west of north. The foundation of the house oriented 5° east of north intruded into the remains of an earlier dwelling, the one situated 30° west of north. This finding revealed that houses changed orientation through time and that they presumably did not face onto established streets.

It has been suggested that since San Luis was never designated a formal pueblo, it may have been exempt from planning regulations. Indeed, when it was initially founded, there may have been little expectation that the settlement would evolve into such a densely populated and economically successful community that would warrant careful urban planning. It is also possible that the Spaniards did not want the Apalachee to know that they had such plans for San Luis.

APALACHEE STRUCTURES

*Artist's conception of a pre-game ceremony in the
council house at San Luis*

The Council House

The dominating architectural feature of San Luis was undoubtedly the large round building covered with a thatch roof that resembled a truncated cone. Known as the council house or lodge, it was located at one end of the town plaza and served as the seat of village government and as a receiving center for delegations from neighboring tribes. It was also the only building in which cacina could be served unless the chief gave express permission otherwise. In mission times, it provided a forum for visiting Spanish officials. If visitors were staying overnight, the council house also functioned as an inn and restaurant. Late in the mission period, Spanish regulations prescribed that visiting Spaniards, blacks, and mulattos could be housed only in the council house and imposed fines on Spaniards and whipping for blacks and mulattos who violated the ordinance.

In mission times, if not before, the council house also served as the village jail and contained stocks where prison-

Artist's rendering of the council house and the chief's house

ers were detained. Regulations issued by Spanish authorities were posted in the council house to ensure that they would be seen by everyone. Such posted regulations were the target of graffiti artists at times. One official visitor found it necessary to issue an edict charging that no one among the natives "be so bold as to smear paint on or scribble on these orders that remain posted in the villages."

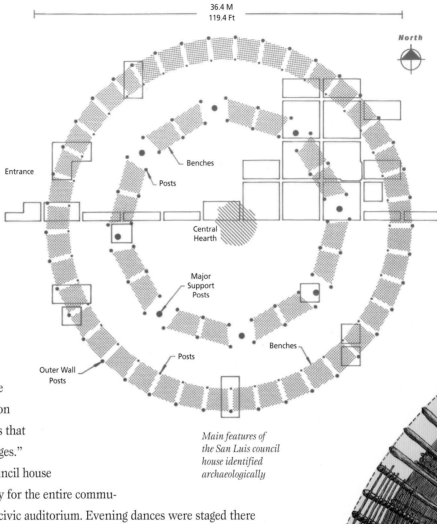

36.4 M
119.4 Ft

North

Entrance

Benches

Posts

Central
Hearth

Major
Support
Posts

Benches

Posts

Outer Wall
Posts

Main features of the San Luis council house identified archaeologically

In the evening the council house became a center of activity for the entire community, playing the role of a civic auditorium. Evening dances were staged there around a large fire kindled in the center of the structure beneath the opening in the thatched roof. These dances continued well into the night and were the natives' major form of entertainment year round. During festivals in pre-Christian times, the dances could last several days. Spaniards curbed such excesses once they had firm control over natives' activities, but deputy governors and official visitors put curbs on friars who restricted the natives' dances excessively. The inner circle of benches enclosed the dance floor and were used by those who watched the dancers. On the east side of the inner circle of compartments, there was a special seat reserved for the principal chief; it was raised above the rest, similar to the throne of European monarchs. The chief's closest advisers sat on either side on benches that probably were raised a little higher than those occupied by ordinary Indians. The chief and other village officials also met in the mornings on those benches to discuss village affairs. During the ceremony preceding the Apalachee ball game, a special bench reserved for the chief was placed behind those of the players. New fires were started between the chief's and players' benches that were to be used only for lighting the chief's tobacco.

Archaeology of the council house revealed that this remarkable example of monumental public architecture measured approximately 120 feet in diameter, making it the largest historic-period Indian building ever found in the Southeast. The structure, which accommodated between 2,000 and 3,000 people, was supported by eight massive pine posts. The interior had a large central hearth and two concentric rows of benches that were divided into small compartments or "cabins."

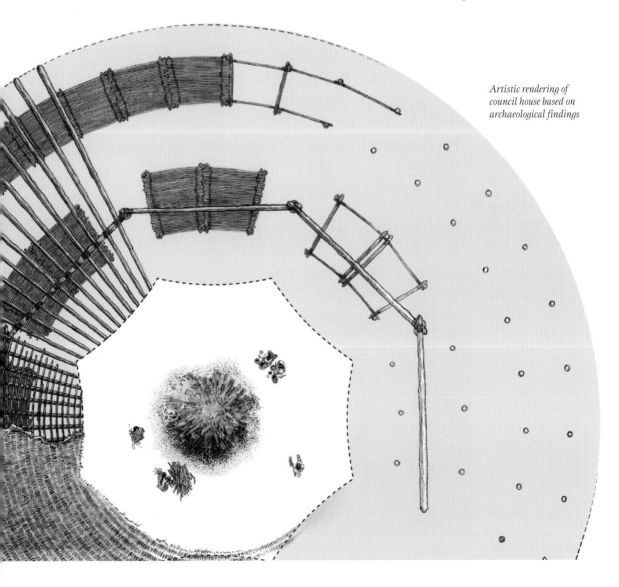

Artistic rendering of council house based on archaeological findings

Each compartment consisted of a raised bench or bed woven of split bamboo or other such material with walls of woven rushes. To provide light and cook individual meals, small fires were kindled on the dirt floor in front of individual compartments. A massive opening or skylight in the center of the roof provided light during the daytime and ventilation for smoke. Dried corncobs smouldered in small pits under the benches to keep insects away.

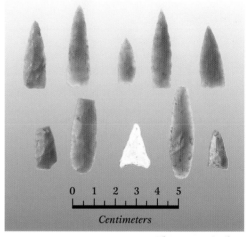

Most of the thousands of artifacts found in the council house were Indian in origin—numerous projectile points, flintknapping residue, and pieces of aboriginal pottery. The relatively small amount of European materials included Hispanic ceramic fragments, glass beads, bells, hardware, and a few pieces of weaponry. Taken as a whole, the assemblage suggests that flintknapping, brewing cacina, and other activities that traditionally took place in council houses continued into the mission period. European materials recovered from the building may be the remains of gifts to Apalachee leaders.

The many projectile points and debitage recovered during the council house excavations reveal that the traditional male activity of flintknapping continued during the mission period.

The Chief's House

Only one native residence thought to belong to a chief has been found at San Luis so far. Such dwellings were probably used not only as a home for a chief and his family but also as a meeting place when a group was small enough to convene in a more intimate place than the council house.

Profiles of alternating posts and smudge pits around the perimeter of the chief's house

The presumed chief's house at San Luis was located on the southern edge of the central plaza, just to the west of the council house. This arrangement made it convenient for the chief's daily meeting in the council house and made him readily accessible to Spanish authorities. The residence measured almost sixty-five feet in diameter, just over one-half the size of the council house. It was similar in appearance to the council house in that it was also round and had a pole framework covered with thatch. There was a central hearth for cooking, and smudge pits lined the interior wall. This building, too, probably had an opening at the top to admit light and allow smoke to escape. The primary architectural differences between this

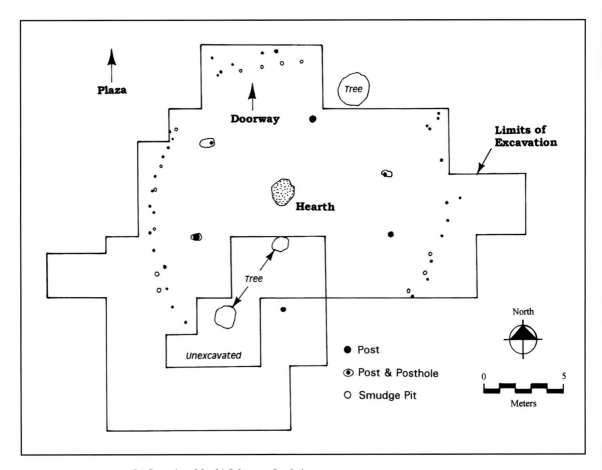

Configuration of the chief's house at San Luis based on archaeological investigations

dwelling and the council house are that the roof of the chief's house had six major support posts rather than eight, and it had no interior benches, indicating that the chief and his family probably slept on mats or hides on the ground.

The materials found in and around this building include native pottery and lithics, and an assortment of European goods such as part of a flintlock, Hispanic ceramics, glass, and beads. There were a particularly large number of faceted quartz crystal beads and

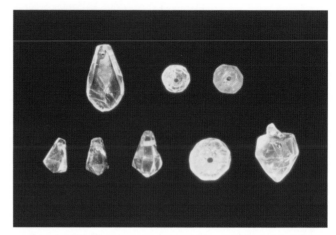

Quartz crystal beads and pendants recovered from excavations of the chief's house at San Luis

At 120 feet in diameter, the council house could accommodate up to 3,000 people.

pendants. The range of exotic goods found is in keeping with the Spanish practice of presenting the chief with gifts in order to reinforce his status and to sustain his allegiance and that of his people. The large number of items made of quartz crystal, which was thought to possess special powers by many southeastern peoples, may be evidence of the dual political and religious power of chiefs.

Commoners' Houses

Commoners' houses associated with San Luis are believed to have been clustered in small hamlets and farmsteads that extended for several miles around the mission center. These houses were considerably smaller than a chief's. The circular buildings typically measured between eighteen and twenty-four feet in diameter and had a simple framework of poles covered with palm-thatch. Although their houses were rather small by modern standards, the Apalachee used them primarily for sleeping and storing their few family possessions. Some Indian houses may have had a few benches or beds consisting of a framework covered with strips of bamboo and a bearskin. A fire built on the dirt floor in the center of the house provided sufficient heat for the Indians to sleep without blankets. This hut was windowless, and the four-foot-high doorway could be closed easily with a mat.

Second in size were leaders' houses, generally about one-half the size (65 feet in diameter) of the council house.

A typical Apalachee home was only 18–24 feet in diameter.

Conjectural view of an
Apalachee hamlet

Storage Shed

For the ordinary Indian the only other domestic structure was an elevated storage building known as a *garita,* where the year's harvest of maize, beans, dried pumpkin, fruits, berries, hickory nuts, and acorns was stored. A dozen beams supported its floor. Venison and fish were smoked and dried as well, but it is not known whether they were stored in the same structure or in a communal one since products of the hunt often were shared.

Artist's concept of an Apalachee garita

EUROPEAN STRUCTURES

The Church

For the residents of San Luis and its hinterland, the church was the most visible symbol of Christianity. Virtually all of the Apalachee living at San Luis accepted the Catholic faith voluntarily, yet they did not give up their reliance on traditional spiritual leaders and healers. And even though most of the Indians did not live on the hilltop, Apalachee and Spaniards alike regularly attended Saturday evening prayers, 11 A.M. Mass on Sundays, services on religious holidays, choir practice, baptisms, marriages, and funeral services in the church. As Christians, the Apalachee wanted to be buried in the cemetery located beneath the church floor.

Archaeological research has revealed that the church was a wooden building faced with vertical planks. Its thatched roof was supported by massive posts, some of which were cypress. The use of cypress is particularly significant since all of the other buildings at San Luis were constructed of pine. While other structures at the site, including the council house, were rebuilt at least once during the almost fifty years that San Luis was occupied, there is no evidence that the cypress church ever deteriorated. In the 1650s, a governor claimed that pine posts at St. Augustine's wooden forts rotted in as little as four years.

Excavation of a major support post associated with the church at Mission San Luis

Artist's conception of the church at Mission San Luis based on archaeological investigations and documentary evidence

The Church at Mission San Luis

Ⓐ Main Altar   Ⓓ Nave & Cemetery

Ⓑ Sacristy   Ⓔ Baptistry

Ⓒ Side Altar   Ⓕ Choir Loft

                 Ⓖ Main Entrance

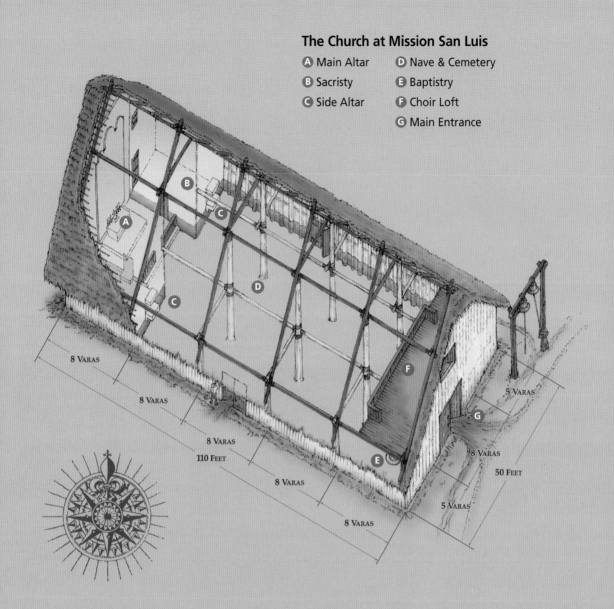

8 VARAS

8 VARAS

8 VARAS

110 FEET

8 VARAS

8 VARAS

5 VARAS

8 VARAS

50 FEET

5 VARAS

The church at San Luis is a fine example of monumental European-style architecture constructed by the Apalachee. Approximately 50 by 110 feet, the church at San Luis was equal in size to the main church in St. Augustine. The long axis of the building ran east to west, as did the *convento*, or friary. Its entrance on the east end opened directly onto the central plaza. Immediately inside the entrance to

The relatively intact base of the baptismal font recovered during excavations in the church

the left, or Gospel side, was the baptistry, where the limestone base of a baptismal font was found intact.

The nave was divided by two rows of support posts that ran lengthwise from the entrance to the sanctuary. There were no benches or pews in mission churches of the seventeenth century, causing some of the Apalachee to have trouble finding their balance in a kneeling position until they became accustomed to it. The floor of the nave also served as the church cemetery where it is thought that between 700 and 900 people were buried.

The sanctuary was at the opposite end of the building from the entrance and was separated from the nave by a wooden railing. A raised clay pad in the center of the sanctuary is the only evidence of where the altar once stood. Plaster found near the altar suggests that the walls at that end of the building were neatly finished, while large pieces of limestone with dressed surfaces found in the sanctuary may be the remains of ornamental columns.

One of the most fascinating revelations about this church was its adherence to a classical proportional system commonly referred to as the Golden Rectangle. After converting archaeological measurements into Spanish *varas* or yards (about thirty-two inches), it became clear that the building was constructed following a scheme that can be traced as far back as Euclid, about 300 B.C. The San Luis church was divided into five longitudinal bays measuring eight varas each. There were also transverse bays; each side bay measured 5 varas wide by 8 varas long. These measurements are in keeping with this classical proportional system using rectangles whose sides are in the relationship of 3 to 5, 5 to 8, 8 to 13, and so forth, and where the sum of any two ratio numbers produces the second number for the next golden relationship. This proportional system became popular again during the Renaissance, and research at San Luis shows that its influence carried over into the architecture of New World frontier settlements.

The overall appearance of the church was undoubtedly impressive in both size and design, but the best indication of its elaborate nature comes from inventories of church furnishings. The thirty-four Florida missions of 1681 contained 183 statues, 444 pictures and paintings, and 69 engravings. There is also a list of the items that were removed from Apalachee Province when it was abandoned in 1704.

Conjectural view of the sanctuary at San Luis

The 1704 Inventory of Church Furnishings from Apalachee Province

The "Report of the silver which churches (?) of the Province of Abalache possessed" includes the following:

Monstrance: seven monstrances, one of silver and the others gilded over.

Plus seven chalices with their patens, plus another three with (theirs?)

Plus three lamps.

Plus eight little containers for administering the viaticum.

Plus seven vessels for storage.

Plus seven crosses of peace.

Plus eleven cruets.

Plus six large crosses.

Plus five thuribles.

Plus three incense boats with the spoons.

Plus 17 chrism vials.

Plus five patens.

Plus two small nails.

Plus another small paten.

Plus another spoon.

Plus 4 small bells and eight halos.

Plus two crowns.

Plus 6 nine-rayed halos for the infant Jesus.

Plus 4 canopies and one altar covering.

Plus six white and black dalmatics.

Plus 13 chasubles of different colors.

Plus 9 copes of different colors.

Plus six altar hangings of different colors.

Plus 3 three short hooded capes.

Plus 4 albs and 2 altar cloths.

Plus one processional cross of the holy Lord, plus another processional cross.

Plus 3 banners.

Plus 4 humeral veils, plus another humeral veil (a shawl-like vestment).

Plus what is in the possession of the Licentiate Soto from that which belonged to the doctrinas of abalache, firstly a purple (?) cope, chasuble, and antependium of silk (?) the same black, plus a red (?) chasuble and antependium, plus a green chasuble, plus two albs, plus two (?) amices, plus a new missal and one for the requiem mass.

Plus a lot of palls, amices, corporals, burses for corporals, and cinctures, which, because the number of all these is great, each thing is not listed [separately].

Colono-ware candlesticks from the San Luis church

An analysis of that inventory, along with the one from 1681, indicates that there were more than enough church furnishings for the celebration of the Mass and to meet other basic needs at the churches of Apalachee. There is little doubt that the church at San Luis contained some of the most elaborate furnishings sent to the province.

Other materials found at the church include large amounts of hardware, a fragment of a bronze church bell, native pottery including Colono-ware candlesticks, objects associated with the cemetery, and Spanish pottery. More than 5,000 Olive Jar fragments were recovered from the sanctuary. These vessels presumably contained water and wine used at Mass.

Daub and burned clay recovered from the friary: (A) whitewashed burned clay; (B) daub with plank or squared timber impression; (C) daub with plant fiber impressions; (D) daub with wattle and lashing impressions.

The Friary

The friary at San Luis was located approximately 106 feet north of the Franciscan church. Although it functioned primarily as a residence for the one or more friars living at San Luis at any given time, it was also used by visiting religious. Others who may have been working in the service of the friars and would have frequented the convento might have included a porter, sacristan, *fiscal* or assistant to the friar, native interpreters, and female Indian servants who laundered clothing, tended the kitchen garden, and cooked. Significant quantities of food were apparently stored in the friary based on the archaeological recovery of large amounts of charred maize and beans remains from the floor of the building.

View of the structures in the religious complex that have been investigated archaeologically

The friary measured approximately 30 by 70 feet, and there is evidence that the interior was separated into rooms. As was the church, this building was European in design and construction. Its main timbers were hewn and fastened together with wrought iron spikes and nails. It was a massive whitewashed wattle and daub building from which three tons of burned clay were removed during excavation.

Large amounts of Indian pottery were found associated with the building, as would be expected with Indian cooks. However, in contrast to the other Hispanic residents at San Luis, the friars apparently had few personal possessions that would show up archaeologically. They presumably had breviaries and other books, along with items such as clothing that would not be easily lost or readily discarded. This would have been in keeping with their vows of poverty and resulted in a material assemblage more reminiscent of a commoner Indian household than that of a Spaniard. Many more imported luxury items were found at the Apalachee chief's residence than at the friary.

Conjectural view of a friar's room in the convento at San Luis

*Conjectural view of the
fort at San Luis*

*Map of Apalachee Bay and the area
around San Luis made by Admiral
Antonio de Landeche during his 1705
reconnaissance of the region*

The Fort

Although the Spanish garrison stationed at San Luis was always small, ranging from twelve to forty-five men, its numbers could be quickly supplemented by *reformados* or civilians who remained on call. The province's military capability was also greatly enhanced by the Apalachee, who probably constituted a formal militia. The Apalachee apparently received some weapons training from the Spaniards; they served as sentries at San Luis, some earned military titles, and they frequently made up most, if not all, of the strike forces sent out from San Luis.

The fort complex at San Luis is the only area of the site for which there is cartographic evidence. In 1705, the year after San Luis was burned and abandoned, Admiral Antonio de Landeche made a reconnaissance of the area accompanied by several soldiers who had been stationed at San Luis. Although his map encompasses a broad area ranging from the northern reaches of the province to Apalachee Bay, the San Luis fort is prominently featured.

The fort complex documented by Landeche was the final one in a series of fortifications constructed at the site. There is every reason to believe that all of them were located in approximately the same location at the north end of the property. The final and most elaborate fort complex was not begun until the 1690s, when Anglo-Creek attacks were imminent. It had four main features: a blockhouse, a palisade, a dry moat, and a covered way.

Landeche described the blockhouse as being "faced with palm posts and backed with clay bricks and above strengthened within and without by a platform of planks." A different account by a Spaniard named Fuentes indicates that the blockhouse had walls of mud that were sheathed with boards about three fingers thick. Archaeological investigations revealed that the San Luis blockhouse was actually wattle and daub. The walls were apparently massive, as one would expect from a building that supported numerous cannon on its roof. More than a half ton of burned clay and daub was recovered from the limited archaeological testing of the building. The blockhouse was whitewashed, as were all of the wattle and daub buildings at San Luis. Although no bricks were found associated with the building as Landeche had indicated, several pieces of charred pine sapling were three fingers thick, as were impressions on pieces of burned daub, just as Fuentes had described.

Although Landeche's description of the building materials appears to be flawed, the dimensions of the fort complex he provided seem to be relatively accurate. The blockhouse was approximately 40 feet wide (north to south) and probably about 70 feet long east to west, although this measurement has yet to be confirmed archaeologically. The limited excavations in the blockhouse demonstrated that the building was divided into rooms, but their respective uses could not be determined. One document describes the blockhouse as having "a guardroom, high and low quarters for the soldiers, a room for the powder, and warehouses for the provisions, its curtains and four bastions with artillery and wall-guns." However, it is likely that provisions, particularly gunpowder, were actually stored in separate structures within the fort complex.

The blockhouse was surrounded by a palisade with four diamond-shaped bastions. The palisade was constructed of wooden posts that extended about 130 feet north to south and 230 feet east to west. It probably stood about eleven feet above the ground surface and was

The size of some charred pine saplings and daub impressions from the fort closely match the Fuentes description of the blockhouse having mud walls that were sheathed with boards about three fingers thick.

*Profiles of major support posts (**right side of photograph**) running along south wall of the blockhouse*

Profile of the south moat showing its stepped configuration

surrounded by a shallow dry moat, three to five feet deep. It was common to plant dry moats with prickly pear cactus or other thorny plants as an added deterrent.

The covered way was a path leading from the southeast corner of the palisade down into the ravine, and it is still clearly visible today. Although there is no archaeological evidence that it was actually covered, the path was defensible from the southeast bastion and provided a way by which soldiers could retain access to water in the ravine if the fort ever came under attack.

In addition to burned clay, archaeological materials recovered from the fort included hardware, weaponry, aboriginal pottery, a rosary, and small quantities of Hispanic pottery, most of which was Olive Jar used to store foods.

Spanish Village

By the 1690s, the Spanish village at San Luis was large. Almost ninety men of arms-bearing age from Apalachee went to the rescue of the colonists in St. August-ine in 1702, so as many as fifty Spanish residences may have been associated with the mission. In fact, other than some civilians living on outlying ranches, most Spaniards resided in this community. In Hispanic homes where Spanish women were present, traditional Iberian lifestyles were probably maintained. However, in keeping with the well-documented pattern of Spanish-Indian intermarriage throughout the rest of New World, many of the Spanish men at San Luis, particu-larly soldiers, probably married Apalachee women.

Documentary evidence suggests that the Hispanic village had the "appearance of a Spanish city" by 1695. Since the town does not appear to have been gridded, the resemblance must have been to medieval Spanish cities which grew in an organic, informal manner. Although the precise extent of the Hispanic village at San Luis is unknown, it probably began in the areas immediately east and northeast of the plaza and extended well beyond the current property boundaries in those directions.

The excavation of three Spanish houses at San Luis has revealed two styles of domestic architecture. One type of residential construction, wattle and daub, was built by digging individual postholes and placing hewn posts directly into the ground. After completing the framework of supports and wattles, the house was covered with daub and whitewashed. The only wattle and daub house excavated to date measured 20 by 30 feet and was partitioned midway down the center. Given the estimated slope of the roof, there was ample room for a second-story loft.

The other type of residential construction, plank and thatch, was built on wooden sills placed directly into the ground. It had a thatch roof and vertical plank walls that were held

Wattle and daub house

Plank and thatch house

together with wrought iron spikes and nails. One of the plank houses measured approximately 12 by 20 feet and was divided in half by a wall. It also had a small wooden plank storage building located behind it. The modest size of this structure indicates that it may have been the residence of a soldier.

A second, larger plank structure situated on the northeast edge of the plaza was also investigated. It appears to have been nearly identical in size and configuration to the wattle and daub dwelling. Although we have no map of the community indicating where specific residents lived, it is probable that an important Spaniard and his family occupied this large house on the plaza. It may even have been home to one of the deputy governors. The materials associated with Spanish households at San Luis are remarkable by virtue of both their quality and quantity. A large number of luxury items were found that had been intentionally discarded, suggesting that these possessions had little or no value to the Spaniards. Imported goods included items of personal adornment, silver spoons, tablewares, and foodstuffs. The materials from the Spanish village speak to the economic prosperity of the community and the thriving trade in which the residents were engaged.

Large amounts of native pottery found in the Spanish
residential area reflect the cultural diversity of the Hispanic
village. Because few artifacts have been found in direct
association with the structures, to date it has been impossible to determine which Spanish houses had Apalachee
women as opposed to Spanish women as their female heads
of household. It appears that everyone took advantage of the
large trash pits that were probably communal in nature.
Perhaps the best indicators of the ethnic makeup of households are the size and location of the structures themselves.
The wealthiest Spanish families, such as the members of the
Florencia family, could afford the largest houses situated in
the most prestigious locations. There is no record that any
of the Florencia men ever married Indian women.

Conceptual view of the Spanish village at San Luis, circa 1700

OTHER ASPECTS OF COMMUNITY ORGANIZATION

Animal Slaughtering and Butchering

While most of the cattle were raised on outlying ranches in Apalachee, there is evidence that animals were slaughtered and butchered in the Spanish village proper. Near several of the dwellings, remains were found that are thought to be from corrals or holding pens. A short distance from these pens were two large borrow pits filled with Spanish domestic refuse, including a large number of cow remains. The skulls were complete enough to identify them as medium-horned cattle, typical of the *criollo* breed introduced throughout much of the Spanish New World. It appears that animals were held in the corrals, then slaughtered and butchered just west of the pens. Their remains were subsequently thrown into the nearby trash pits.

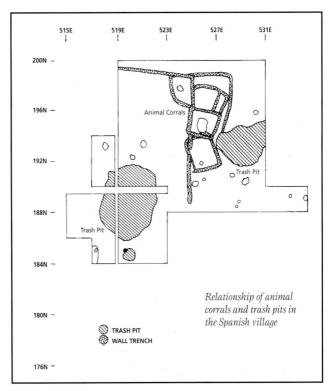

Relationship of animal corrals and trash pits in the Spanish village

Trash Disposal

Trash pits at other Spanish colonial sites like St. Augustine typically contain just a few days' refuse, but trash deposits at San Luis are unusually large and often filled with thousands of artifacts. While some sheet midden does accumulate across the site, ongoing construction at the mission center provided an ideal situation for trash disposal. Near every wattle and daub structure at the site, large clay mines or borrow pits were excavated by native laborers. These are highly irregular pits, the largest of which measured over 26 feet in diameter and more than 6 feet deep. This size is consistent with the amount of clay needed to build a structure from which tons of burned clay are later recovered archaeologically. Once these massive pits were dug, they presented an immediate hazard to the community, particularly to small children and animals. Most were apparently filled with trash rather quickly as pieces of pottery from the same vessel have been found at the top and bottom of the same pit.

Excavating large clay mine later filled with trash in the Spanish village

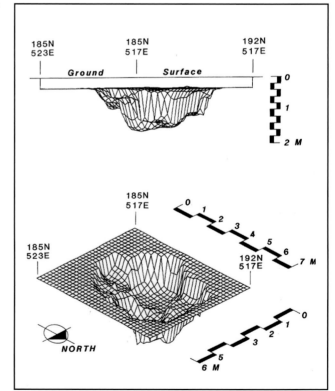

Computer-simulated diagram of trash pit configuration

Service Area

Extensive archaeological testing south and southwest of the plaza revealed a diverse assortment of Apalachee artifacts but no structural remains. This part of the site was probably a service area for those Apalachee who worked on the hilltop but did not live there. Although most Apalachee commoners lived in the low-lying areas around the site where they could tend their fields, many were involved in construction projects or other types of service to the chiefs or members of the Spanish community near the mission center.

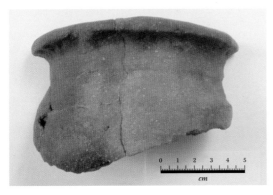

One of the partially reconstructed vessels recovered from the waster pit

It is believed that the extensive borrow pits found on this part of the site were used for mining clay and processing daub during construction. The diverse lithic assemblage from this area probably resulted from a number of activities including butchering and preparing hides, while the native pottery likely represents various types of food preparation. Most intriguing was the discovery of a large surface hearth, measuring 13 feet in diameter, and a nearby waster pit. There were no food remains found in the hearth, indicating that it was not used for cooking. This finding, however, is consistent with the interpretation that it was used for firing native pottery. The associated waster pit was unlike typical trash pits at San Luis in that it was filled almost exclusively with pottery. It contained a minimum of 71 and a maximum of 223 individual vessels. These features provide the first direct evidence of pottery manufacturing at a Florida mission.

Foodways

Foodways encompass not only the foods people eat but the manner in which they are procured, prepared, and served. Cross-cultural studies have demonstrated that this aspect of daily life is among the most conservative and slow to change, and the availability of preferred foods has a strong influence on a person's sense of well being.

Spaniards in the New World often judged territories not only on the basis of natural wealth, such as gold and silver, but on their suitability for raising domesticated plants and animals of Mediterranean origin. One of the most frequently cited examples from Spanish Florida of a general unhappiness with locally available foods is the testimony of a soldier stationed in St. Augustine in 1573. Despite the fact that perfectly nutritious resources were bountiful on the Atlantic coastal plain, they were not the preferred foods of Spaniards. The soldier stated that provisions were issued sporadically and that "when there was nothing they ate herbs, fish and other scum and vermin."

Diet

Basic Mediterranean staples included wine, olive oil, olives, and wheat. Spaniards also raised and consumed large quantities of livestock—sheep, cattle, and pigs—which were

Shipping Manifests

The following excerpts from shipping manifests show some of the exports sent from Apalachee to Havana by various entrepreneurs including Diego de Florencia, one of San Luis's wealthiest traders:

Date of Arrival in Havana	Cargo
26 March 1674	150 hides; 150 arrobas (3800 lbs.) of tallow
21 January 1681	700 hides; 50 tercios of tallow, each one containing 4 arrobas (5070 lbs.)
10 March 1682	150 fanegas (237 bushels) of corn and beans; 100 arrobas (2536 lbs.) of tallow; 40 jugs of lard; 190 hides
17 June 1685	100 chickens; 110 hams; 35 jugs of lard; 300 deerskins; 28 fanegas (44 bushels) of corn; 60 arrobas (1410 lbs.) of tar
16 June 1686	Beans, corn, and lard
12 July 1694	75 chickens; 82 arrobas (2080 lbs.) of meat

preferred by most over fishes and seafood. However, as in all Catholic countries, most Spaniards ate fish on all Fridays, on Wednesdays in Lent and Advent, and on other Ember days as well.

As one of the most fertile areas in Florida, Apalachee Province provided ideal conditions for Spanish colonists. Not only were they able to produce many of their favorite foods for local consumption, but San Luis is the only Spanish colonial community in La Florida where European-introduced livestock, particularly beef and pork, were eaten more than any other meat. Spaniards imported olive oil, wine, and other Mediterranean foods which could not be locally produced.

By the 1670s, agricultural exports became the economic cornerstone of San Luis and Apalachee was known as a breadbasket to Spanish Florida. However, San Luis traders preferred selling their goods in Havana, where they received higher prices and payment in cash and could purchase exotic items from around the world.

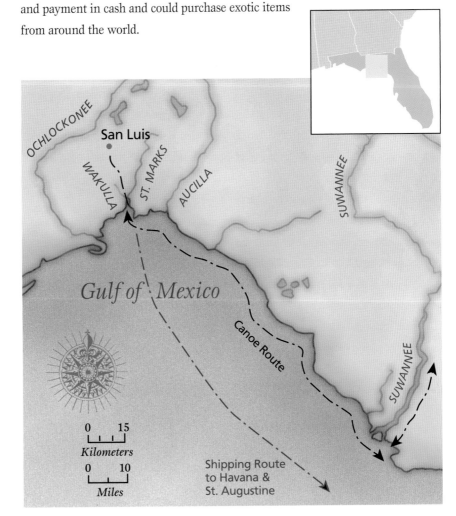

Shipping routes from Apalachee to Havana and St. Augustine

Although Spaniards took advantage of some foods that were native to Florida, including deer, corn, beans, fish, and turtles, the successful introduction of Spanish foodstuffs largely overshadowed their use of local resources. Maize, beans, and squash were the staples for the Apalachee as they were for all Mississippian cultures. As they crossed the province, the chroniclers of the de Soto expedition remarked on the extensive fields of these crops and others. In fact, de Soto's decision to winter in Apalachee was based largely on the abundance of stored foods.

Traditional Apalachee plant foods also included maypop, cabbage palm, palm berry, knotweed, several types of starchy roots, acorns, hickory nuts, persimmon, wild grape, wild or cherry plum, blackberry, and yaupon holly. The latter was used to make the Indian tea known as cacina or black drink. The Apalachee also used tobacco and a tobacco substitute or extender, and they gathered a considerable number of plants for medicinal use but little is known about them.

Locally procured animals included deer, bear, panther, turkey, rabbit, squirrel, raccoon, opossum, geese, and various wild ducks. Buffalo could also be found to the west near present-day Marianna. Bear was the most highly prized meat and provided cooking oil, which also came from acorns and hickory nuts.

While Spaniards traditionally stored their meat "on the hoof," the Apalachee were great hunters. A communal hunt was carried out in January as the fields were being cleared for planting. Hunters surrounded the burning fields and adjacent woods as dried grass, weeds, and debris from the previous year's crops were set ablaze. Fleeing deer, rabbits, and birds were all easily brought down. Afterward, hunters entered the woods that had just been cleared of underbrush in pursuit of bear and panthers that had fled from the fire. The product of this hunt was brought to the chief who divided it among the people. He set aside the share of the skins that was owed to him, which included all of the bear and panther skins.

With missionization came the introduction of a wide variety of new food sources. Since the Apalachee worked as laborers on Spanish ranches and farms and as servants tending gardens and cooking, they quickly became familiar with plants such as peaches, pomegranates, quinces, wheat, barley, peas, chickpeas, figs, watermelon, and new superior strains of tobacco. Prior to the arrival of Europeans, dogs were the only domestic animal known to the Apalachee. They soon learned animal husbandry, first with chickens and hogs and later with cattle and horses. Although sheep and goats were introduced into Spanish Florida by Pedro Menéndez de Avilés, neither fared well in the subtropical climate. Their remains are scant in the archaeological record, and they are almost never mentioned in historical accounts.

It is difficult to tell exactly how many Apalachee had access to livestock. Although there is documentary evidence to indicate that some individual natives and Apalachee communities had cattle, these occurrences may have been rare. In those cases, Indians may have kept livestock more as an investment than as a food source.

Multiple lines of evidence suggest that the Apalachee's access to livestock may have been restricted and reserved primarily for native leaders. Bishop Calderón remarked in 1675 that the diet of Christianized Indians "consists of porridge which they make of corn with ashes, pumpkins, beans which they call *frijoles*, with game and fish from the rivers and lakes which the well-to-do ones can afford." Preliminary isotope analysis of skeletal remains from the cemetery at San Luis indicates that only one Apalachee received most of his protein from meat, and he was believed to be a man of high social standing since he was buried in a coffin close to the altar. The recovery of cow and pig remains from the Apalachee chief's house at San Luis provides additional evidence that livestock was available to Indian leaders.

Food Preparation

Maize was a year-round staple for the Apalachee. It was cooked in a number of ways: as a lye-hominy porridge made with ashes, in little cakes made of cornmeal, in a thin gruel known as *onsla*, in a thick gruel similar to the Mexican *atole*, and as toasted or parched corn flour for use while traveling. Meat from the hunt was typically dried and smoked. Documentary evidence suggests that the Apalachee maintained significant stores of dried meat, particularly vension.

Spanish methods of food preparation and preservation (particularly jerked beef and pork) were not much different from those of the Apalachee. Their staple meal was stew or porridge made with whatever was available, including meat, fish and vegetables. This method was seen as a way to extend meat that in some areas was in short supply. However, at places such as San Luis, where beef and pork were abundant, they may have roasted their meat at times.

Replica pottery used in the preparation and storage of cacina: a flat-bottom bowl for roasting leaves, a globular vessel for brewing, and a large storage jar

Food Service

The liquid-based Apalachee gruels and porridges, as well as the Spanish stews or *gachas*, dictated that the primary cooking pots be hollowwares. Traditional Apalachee pottery was made in a relatively limited range of vessel forms. The basic shapes were bowls and jars, both of which were made with a variety of rim, neck, and base treatments. They were all relatively large and intended for communal purposes. For specialized activities, such as making black drink, a series of pots were used. A flat-bottomed bowl or *cazuela* was used for roasting the yaupon leaves, which were then transferred into a globular jar with water for brewing. Once finished, it was poured into a jar with a restricted neck for storage.

*Leon Check Stamped (**top row**) and Lamar Complicated Stamped sherds (**bottom row**) from San Luis*

Most Apalachee pottery found at San Luis is undecorated and tempered with grog, or small pieces of pottery, and sand. The decorated pottery is typically stamped and falls into two broad "types," Lamar Complicated Stamped and Leon Check Stamped, both of which include a number of design "varieties."

Traditional Spanish ceramic cooking pots also came in two basic forms: globular *pucheros* and flat-bottomed cazuelas or stewpans. Spaniards used copper and iron pots as well. However, at most Spanish colonial sites where there was a vigorous native ceramic tradition, Spaniards relied heavily on Indian vessels for cooking. This was certainly the case at San Luis where there is little evidence of Spanish cooking pots but an abundance of native ceramics throughout the site. Not only did these work just as well, but they were probably preferred by the native women who did most of the cooking for Apalachee and Spaniards alike.

An important difference between the two pottery traditions is that while the Apalachee did not use any individual dishes or tablewares, Spaniards considered them to be an integral part of food service. Hispanic residents at San Luis spared little expense to import highly decorated plates, bowls, pitchers, and other tablewares from Spain, Mexico, and the Orient. Unlike cooking vessels, which stayed out of sight, tablewares were used in a prominent way and no doubt reinforced the Spaniards' cultural identity and status.

Although the Apalachee never made individual dishes prior to European contact, they became adept at it during the mission period. When imported pottery was in short supply, the Apalachee made European-style plates, bowls,

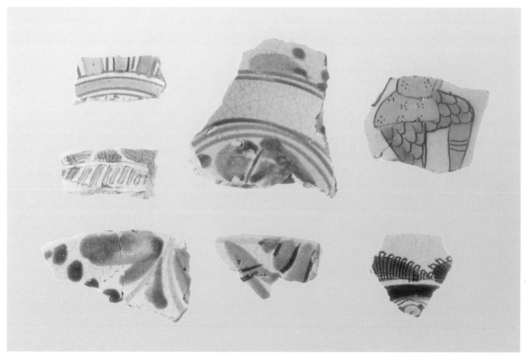

Majolica types frequently recovered from the Spanish village at San Luis. **Left to right:**
(top) *Abó′ Polychrome; San Luis Polychrome; Abó′ Polychrome;* ***(middle)*** *Castillo Polychrome;* ***(bottom)*** *San Luis Blue on White; Fig Springs Polychrome; Puebla Polychrome.*

These replica Colono-wares vessels are based on fragments found at San Luis.

and other vessels for the Spaniards. Known as Colono-wares in Spanish Florida, these tablewares were manufactured using aboriginal ceramic technology, including coil construction and open hearth firing.

Colono-wares at San Luis are thought to have been locally made since the paste, construction, and firing methods are the same as those used for traditional Apalachee pottery. Although Apalachee women were skilled at making these tablewares, there is no evidence that they ever used these vessels themselves. The only native women who likely used Colono-wares at San Luis were those married to Spanish men, since this pottery is found almost exclusively in Spanish areas of the site, particularly in the Hispanic village.

OTHER ASPECTS
OF MATERIAL LIFE

Clothing and Adornment

European clothing was one of the gifts from Spanish officials to elite Apalachee women and men at an early period. Most if not all of the principal chiefs and inijas probably wore some articles of Spanish clothing for their prestige value, if for no other reason. Apalachee leaders who adopted completely hispanicized names, such as Alonso Pastrana or Juan Mejía, probably also preferred to dress in Spanish-style clothing. Even common laborers began to obtain blanket-like ponchos and other garments made of coarse fabrics once the labor draft was imposed in 1647.

However, as late as 1675, two generations after missionization had begun, most Apalachee men still wore only a breechclout made of leather or plaited straw. Women dressed only in a skirt made from Spanish moss that covered them from waist to knee. This clothing probably began to change on a large scale only with the expansion of the Spanish community in the 1680s and 1690s, when many more goods were imported to meet the demands of this burgeoning sector of the population. Spaniards were notorious for their ostentation and lavish displays of material wealth. In fact, sumptuary laws passed in Spain in the sixteenth and seventeenth centuries to curb this behavior included prohibitions

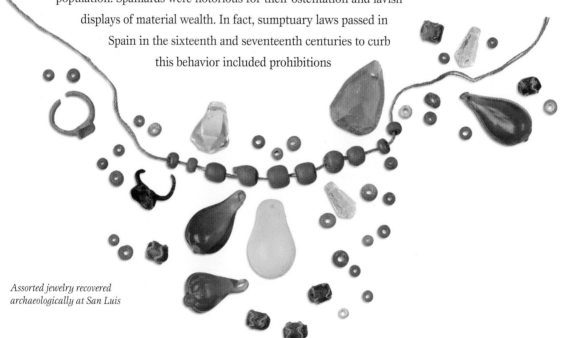

Assorted jewelry recovered archaeologically at San Luis

*Jet higas or protective amulets recovered from San Luis exhibit considerable variation in their size and shape. The largest of these higas (**top row, center**) is 3 cm long.*

against some fabrics such as silk and brocades and limits on the number of domestic servants one could have.

Shows of material wealth may have been nowhere more pronounced at San Luis than in the Spaniards' clothing and jewelry. Examples of fine cloth, elaborate buttons, embroidery beads, silver sequins, pendants, beads, amulets, and rings for both children and adults have been found in the Spanish village.

Exposure to Spanish-style clothing and accessories apparently had a significant influence on the Apalachee population who, by the end of the seventeenth century, were dressing in a predominantly European fashion. The French in Mobile described the Apalachee who migrated there in 1704 as dressing like Europeans. The women wore cloaks and silk skirts, and the men were dressed in overcoats. While this may have been their Sunday best, a transition had clearly taken place.

In addition to adopting European clothing, Apalachee hair styles also changed in keeping with Spanish styles. At the time of contact, both Apalachee men and women wore their hair long. During the mission period, men were expected to cut their hair at the time of their baptism as an indication that they had become "civilized." Although the women were not expected to cut their hair when baptized, Apalachee women were described by the Mobile chroniclers as having their hair woven into one or two plaits that hung down their backs like that of Spanish girls. If their hair was very long, it was folded up to the middle of their backs and tied with a ribbon.

Although there is no indication that chiefs continued to use any of the late prehistoric insignia such as copper breastplates during the mission period, they did use certain types of ornamentation to distinguish themselves from commoners. Locally made shell bead bracelets worn around the neck, upper arm, and leg may have served this purpose. But it is believed that European items given to the chiefs from the governor, such as fancy canes and staffs, as well as other imported objects, were held in great esteem. The status of all of the principal chiefs was further reinforced by Spaniards who addressed them as noblemen, using the title "Don" before their name. This was the equivalent of the English "Sir" used by those who have been knighted or have inherited a family title of nobility.

Body Painting

One traditional area of personal adornment that the Apalachee continued well into mission times was body painting. Documents indicate that Apalachee men painted their faces and bodies on ceremonial occasions and for war, and probably on other occasions as well. Ball game players probably stained their bodies with a color or colors representing the dominant clan of their village. For example, when a messenger from San Luis went to another village to challenge them to a ball game, he went in the guise of a raccoon. He wore a raccoon tail, painted his face red, and stained his body black with raylike streaks through it. San Luis's Fray Juan de Paiva said that the courier "looked like the devil himself." He also noted that the players who considered themselves to be descended from dark strong animals such as the wolf, panther, and bear painted themselves black, while their rivals painted themselves other colors representing different animals such as the deer and fox.

Body painting was another native practice that Spaniards would have considered "uncivilized." The degree to which ordinary body painting continued under such pressure is not known, but their use of warpaint did survive. In 1700, St. Augustine's pastor noted that when the Apalachee went to war, "they dress themselves elaborately, after their usage, painted all over with red ochre and with their heads full of multicolored feathers."

There is no explicit indication that the Apalachee tattooed their faces and bodies as did other Florida natives like the Timucua and Tocobaga. However, there was something distinctive about their appearance that enabled Spaniards and blacks in St. Augustine, who had only casual contact with them, to distinguish them immediately from other Indians.

Study of Apalachee man with raccoon body painting by Edward Jonas. Reproduced courtesy of the artist.

Weapons

There is no doubt that the introduction of metal weapons and firearms changed the Apalachee's perception of warfare and their ability to protect themselves against Europeans. At the time of their first encounter with Spaniards, the most commonly used weapon was the bow and arrow. War clubs or cudgels made of

Archaeological evidence of firearms from chief's house at San Luis

wood and hatchets or tomahawks with stone blades hafted into wooden handles were used for hand-to-hand combat. Their favorite weapon for taking scalps was a sharpened reed.

Apalachee's bows and arrows did prove effective against Spanish chain mail. In an experiment, de Soto's soldiers had a captive Apalachee shoot an arrow through four layers of chain mail placed over a basket. However, bows and arrows were still no match for Spanish weapons.

After contact, the Apalachee began using iron and steel knives for scalping, and iron hatchets became a favorite weapon for one-on-one fighting. Initially, the Spaniards restricted Indian access to firearms and gave them to only a few leaders. But by the 1670s, a considerable number of Apalachee had acquired firearms from traders and were familiar with their use and maintenance. Eventually native warriors at sites such as San Luis became part of a formally trained militia whose leaders enjoyed Spanish military commissions and carried firearms. Historical evidence is borne out archaeologically by the remains of gun parts, lead shot, and gunflints that were found at both the Apalachee council house and the chief's house at San Luis.

In 1677, a largely Apalachee force of 190 warriors, many from San Luis, mounted an expedition against a Chisca village on the Choctawhatchee River.

Thirty of them were armed with harquebuses which they used effectively during their assault. In 1700, a pastor in St. Augustine remarked that, although the Apalachee still relied primarily on the bow and arrow, "they use firearms as do the Spaniards and they maintain their arms as well as do the best trained officers."

Seventeenth-Century Weapons

The probate inventory of a Spanish captain made in the mid-seventeenth century includes the following weapons, which may have been typical of ordnance owned by soldiers:

two old sword belts

a tin-covered fire case with 8 powder flasks

a carrying case for a ram-rod

a little pocket pistol

an harquebus and powder flasks

a cutlass

a shoulder-belt with its cutlass

a shoulder-belt with its waist belt

Tools

Prior to contact with the Spaniards, the principal raw materials used by the Apalachee for the manufacture of tools were wood, stone, bone, deer antler, and shell. They used stone axes for cutting down trees and hoes made of wood, stone, or shell for their fields and gardens.

As with weapons, many traditional Apalachee tools were found to be inferior to metal counterparts that the Spaniards introduced. Spaniards imported a range of iron tools and hardware including mattock-like hoes, machetes, sickles, axes, adzes, awls, chisels, drills, hammers, knives, saws, nails, spikes, hinges, padlocks, and latches. Except for awls, adzes, hoes, axes, knives, hatchets, and chisels, few of these tools ever became the property of Indians. The Apalachee became so familiar with European building techniques and tools that during his 1675 visitation Bishop Calderón described them as "great carpenters as evidenced in the construction of their wooden churches which are large and painstakingly wrought."

One of the best sources of information about the types of tools that were available in seventeenth-century Spanish Florida is the auction inventory from the Asile wheat farm. In addition to the land and buildings, slaves, livestock, tools, and furnishings were sold.

The value placed on tools is evidenced by the fact that they are almost never recovered archaeologically. Several knives found in the Spanish village at San Luis appear to be kitchen or dinner knives. The only other examples of tools recovered at the site are a chisel from the convento and two large iron knives, one from the Apalachee service area and the other associated with a native burial. The knife blades and tangs were intact, but their wooden or bone handles had disintegrated. Hardware was also highly prized, as attested to by several documented instances of nails being salvaged from abandoned or destroyed buildings and ships.

Auction Inventory from the Asile Farm

Plus four pesos for a table of boards.

Plus, for a used grindstone, four pesos, rather, eight pesos [sic].

Plus six pesos for six benches [made of boards].

Plus one peso for a kitchen (or stable) oil-lamp.

Plus four pesos, a machete, a drill, and a short, thick goad.

Plus six pesos for three wooden beds.

Plus one hundred and seventeen pesos for thirteen used iron ploughshares

(could also be interpreted as iron grates or railings).

Plus eight pesos for four used hoes (could possibly be shovels).

Plus twenty-one pesos for seven used axes.

Plus thirty-three pesos for eleven sickles.

Plus two pesos for an old bottle case.

Plus two pesos for three chisels.

Plus five pesos for two hammers.

Plus four pesos for four drills.

Plus nine pesos for three hand axes.

Plus five pesos for two saws and one handsaw.

Plus fourteen pesos for four planes (zepillos) and two jointing-planes.

Plus five pesos for two used tablecloths.

Plus two pesos for four hooks for eels (or sea bass).

Plus two pesos for a pewter plate.

Plus four pesos for two machetes.

Plus five pesos for two chocolate stones (used for grinding chocolate beans).

Plus twenty-four pesos for eight used iron spurs (or goads).

Plus eight pesos for two iron chains.

RELIGION

Christianity and the Apalachee

The missionization of the Apalachee was considered a success by both Church and Crown. Spaniards relied heavily on the Apalachee missions to secure their tenure in the western hinterland and to provide provisions for the rest of Spanish Florida. The Church's primary objective was to save the souls of their native charges, whom they thought of as children. By the early 1670s, Apalachee Province had a series of well-established missions. It produced a significant surplus of agricultural goods to meet the needs of the colonists, and its people were described as thoroughly Christianized.

However, the best indicators of the success of missionization are found in the deeds and actions of the Apalachee themselves. Conversion to Roman Catholicism had a profound effect on many aspects of their lives from baptism to funeral rites. As Catholics, the Apalachee at death chose to be buried in the consecrated ground beneath the floor of the church. As many as 900 people may be buried in the cemetery at San Luis. Some of these people may be chiefs from outlying villages who wanted to be buried in the main church at the mission capital. As it did in elite prehistoric Apalachee burials, rank also had its privileges among deceased missionized Apalachee, although burial during the mission period followed a distinctly Christian pattern. All of the burials were extended with their hands

folded across their chest. Elite members of Apalachee society
buried at San Luis are found closest to the altar placed in
discrete pits. Three of the burials near the altar are interred
with their heads to the west, opposite all of the other burials
in the cemetery. This orientation was usually reserved for
friars and attests to the high social or economic rank of these
individuals in mission-era Apalachee society. They may have
been native rulers, parish interpreters, or individuals of
equivalent standing. Some of the people interred near the
altar are also buried in pine coffins and are accompanied
by grave offerings. Although the Catholic Church may have
discouraged this practice, the Apalachee continued their
native custom of including grave items with the deceased
for use in the afterlife. The most elaborate artifact from the
cemetery is a quartz crystal cross believed to have been made
by a native artisan.

Commoners were also buried beneath the floor of the
church. However, most of these burials were located away
from the altar and were placed on top of one another with
apparently no concern about disturbing previous burials.
None had a coffin burial, and few of the people buried
away from the altar had objects interred with them.

Religious conversion also had an impact on social and
military aspects of daily life at the mission. *Cofradías* or
religious brotherhoods were common in Spain and in Spanish
American settlements alike. They had a number of functions
that included financial and material support of the church
and acts of charity to the poor or infirm. They were also
renowned for their colorful processions on religious holidays.
The Apalachee at San Luis formed at least one cofradía
dedicated to Our Lady of the Rosary.

The Apalachee's religious conviction was put to the
ultimate test during the British-Creek attacks that led to the

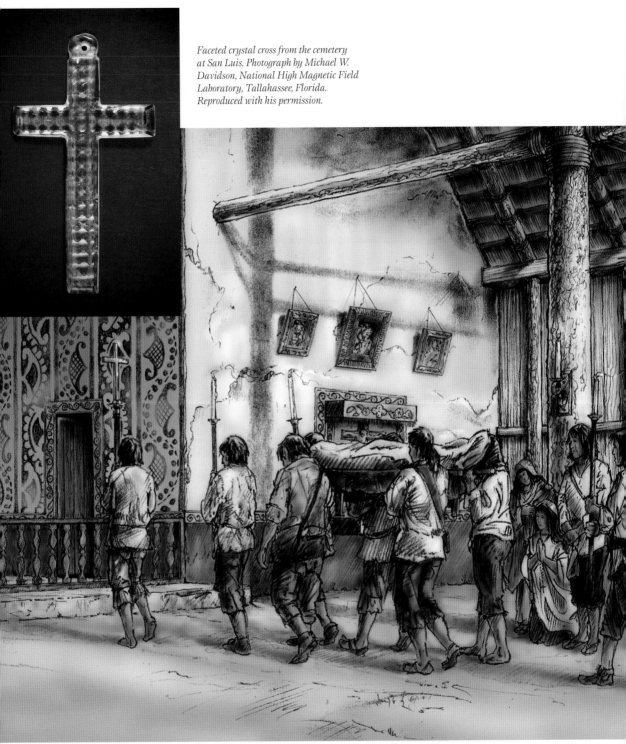

Faceted crystal cross from the cemetery at San Luis. Photograph by Michael W. Davidson, National High Magnetic Field Laboratory, Tallahassee, Florida. Reproduced with his permission.

Artist's rendering of a funeral procession inside the church at San Luis

abandonment of the missions. Most Apalachee and Spaniards fled the province to avoid enslavement or death, but several Apalachee men from San Luis were captured and suffered a lingering death at the stake professing their faith. The king of Spain was so impressed by the Apalachee's acceptance of their fate that he suggested to the Vatican that they be considered for canonization as martyrs.

Those Apalachee who migrated to Mobile after they were forced to abandon their traditional homeland were described by a French priest as being devout Catholics who clamored for service. Father Alexander Huvé wrote to a friend, "You cannot believe the trouble the Apalachee are causing us. They are constantly asking for sacraments, and we cannot understand them anymore than we can make ourselves understood."

There is every reason to believe that the Apalachee's conversion to Catholicism was sincere and resulted in some profound behavioral changes. They participated in church activities, they followed religious observances, and they lived by the Christian calendar in communities where church bells marked out their days. However, they also continued to rely on some traditional spiritual leaders and beliefs throughout the mission period.

Traditional Apalachee Religion

Most of what is known directly about the Apalachee's religious beliefs derives from the Apalachee ball game manuscript written by San Luis's Fray Juan de Paiva in 1676. The manuscript describes the game itself, its purposes, its associated rituals, and some of the myths related to the origin of the game. Presumably, what French observers recorded about the coastal Timucua's worship of the sun and moon generally applies to the Apalachee as well. Head chiefs likely were the supreme religious authorities. They probably claimed special ties with the sun-god as did those of other southeastern tribes. There is no mention of images or idols being associated with Apalachee religious practice, but since idols were used among their neighbors, it is likely that they were a feature of Apalachee religion as well. The Apalachee had religious specialists or shamans whose activities included healing, divining, and prescribing curative herbs. They also blessed crop production, hunting, and fishing and were responsible for the casting and lifting of spells. Shamans also functioned as midwives.

Artist's conception of Juan de Paiva

Juan de Paiva, pastor at San Luis, wrote a
description of the ball game and his perception of
its evils as part of his campaign to stop the game.
Two native interpreters provided many of the
details about the origins and religious practices
associated with the ball game.

The religious functions of the Apalachee ball game may not have been obvious to the casual observer or something that the Indians readily revealed to outsiders, particularly to Europeans. The earliest description of that game, written by a friar in 1630 and probably based on the version of the game played in western Timucua, gives no hint at all that the game had religious implications. Similarly, a friar's questions for hearing the confessions of game players in general, written almost a generation earlier in 1614, do not imply that the friar perceived overtones of religious beliefs from pre-Christian times. The questions were for eastern Timucuans who played a game that was distinct from the Apalachee one. All but one of his questions are similar to those that a priest might address to a modern confessant he recognized as a sports enthusiast or a gambler. Did you cheat or lie to win the game? Have you lost everything you own? Even a last doubtful question has a potentially modern ring to it, if one substitutes "steroid" for "herb": Have you taken some herb and rubbed your hands with it with the desire of winning because of it?

The first mention of the Apalachee game per se dates from the 1657 visitation when natives complained that some friars were prohibiting the game. The record does not specify the reason for the prohibition. It may have been the game's violence or the intense and extensive wagering that the game spawned. The governor, in response, forbade friars from prohibiting the game. Only a generation later did another friar attempt to ban the game.

Father Juan de Paiva began campaigning against the game in 1676 especially because of its link to pre-Christian native religious observances, particularly the rituals associated with raising the goal post and the identification of the post with the god of rain and thunder. He also objected to the wagering, violence, and sexual license associated with the game. Fray Paiva had been tolerant of the game as late as early 1675 when he was pastor at San Luis. However, when Bishop Gabriel Díaz Vara Calderón visited the mission and saw the violence associated with a tamer boys' version of the game, he outlawed the adult ball game. Although Paiva interceded successfully with the bishop to lift the ban, the friar began to observe the game more critically. Probably in response to a suggestion from Paiva, two native interpreters based at San Luis conducted an inquiry into the origins of the game, as well as the ceremonies and customs associated with it. The fact that the native interpreters had to consult with others about the origin myth suggests that some oral traditions were already being lost to a new generation or that this was reserved information.

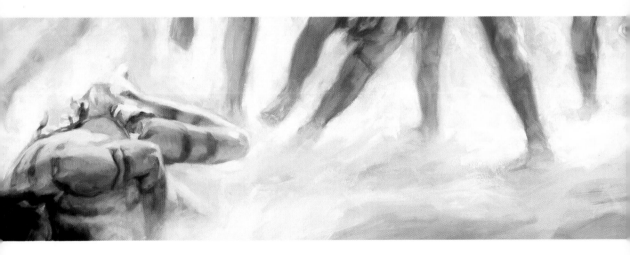

The interpreters incorporated their findings in a report, referred to usually as the *cuaderno* or notebook, that was critical of the game. Influenced by their study and his own observations, Paiva became convinced that the game was evil in itself and in its consequences. Inspired by this change of heart, he wrote a treatise condemning the game, based largely on the interpreter's findings but incorporating his own observations as well. And after composing an initial draft, he added new arguments to win wider support for the game's prohibition throughout the province as well as in his own parish. It is this final treatise that is known as the ball game manuscript.

This drawing of the goal post is based on a sketch from Fray Juan de Paiva's manuscript.

The Rules of the Game

The basic equipment for playing the game was a tall goal post surmounted by an eagle's nest, a stuffed eagle standing in the nest with a few shells under its feet, and a small, hard buckskin ball filled with hardened clay. The number of players on each of the two teams varied in accordance with the size of the villages playing. Forty or fifty players to a side appear to have been typical in 1676, but the 1630 description noted, "It is played 50 against 50 and 100 against 100 in conformity with the people who show up," reflecting the larger populations of some villages in that era. Only the foot was used to propel the ball toward the goal. One point was awarded each time the ball struck the post. If a player kicked the ball in the eagle's nest, his team gained two points. The first team to earn eleven points won.

Both the 1630 and the 1676 descriptions attest that the games drew large crowds to the town's central plaza where it was played "because of its being attractive to watch." The 1630 account described the plaza for the Apalachee game as being "for this purpose alone large, level (*llana*) and hardened (*empedrada*)." Empedrada literally means "paved with stones" or "cobbled," but it can also mean dappled as in "flecked with clouds."

The 1630 account also described the goal post as a thick, tall log placed in the middle of the field. The account included a miniaturized version of the same drawing later depicted in the 1676 manuscript. The post had the appearance of a flattened Christmas tree. Its triangular shape appears to represent a framework of some sort.

Raising the Goal Post

Elaborate rituals were established for setting up the goal post. Five sassafras pegs were attached to the converging sides of the triangular framework. Once the basic framework had been assembled, the crowning nest was put in place facing east. The pegs were then attached with some type of decorations apparently tied to them. The hole for raising the pole and the eagle atop the pole had to face the setting sun. Only grapevines were used in raising the pole in commemoration of one of the tests the game's mythic patron had endured.

For some time before the post was raised and put into place, warriors danced around it to the sound of a drum, howling or barking occasionally like dogs and wolves. To raise the post, groups of men and women pulled on the vines from different sides. The warriors continued their dance while the pole was being raised and were joined by six women and six additional warriors. No woman could remain in her house during this ceremony. A young unmarried woman, carrying the short lacrosse-like stick used in the women's ball game, performed an unspecified ceremony beneath the pole in memory of Nicotaijulo, mother of the game's mythic patron, Nicoguadca, who was identified with the god of thunder and rain and to whom the pole was dedicated. As the pole was about to be set in place, the usinulo, or "beloved son" of the chief, made a ceremonious salute of reverence to the pole. Placing his hands together as in prayer, the usinulo pronounced the word *gua* three times, poured out a cup of cacina in honor of the pole, and performed other unspecified rituals. A final rule stipulated that a human skull or scalp be placed at the foot of the post in honor of the game's legendary founder, Ytonanslac. Fray Paiva considered these rituals to be idolatrous worship of the pole and of the god of lightning and rain with which the pole and the game were associated.

Pre-Game Rituals

The ritual for raising the pole also prescribed that a dance be held on the night before the event. For that evening alone, the usual taboos governing sexual conduct were suspended for both married and single women. During the dance the chief went about begging the women not to resist any advances made to them in order to prevent their husbands and brothers and the village's leaders from losing everything they owned. This was a reference to the natives' custom of making substantial bets on the game's outcome.

The pre-game dance and rituals had to be performed on the night before the game or the village team would lose, according to native belief. At sunset or soon thereafter the ball players assembled in the council house. Special hollowed-out log benches without legs were brought in and placed so that the players would be facing the direction of the village that they were going to play against the following day. If the village was to the north, the benches were placed on the south side so that the players could sit facing north. A drummer, a rattle shaker, and all of the women also faced toward the opponents' village because they believed that if they turned their backs their village's team would lose the game. The dancers exited by the south side, letting out whoops and indicating the direction of the competitors' village with their arms extended.

A special bench was reserved for the chief behind the players' hollowed-out benches. New fires were started between the chief's and players' benches that were to be used only for lighting the chief's tobacco. To achieve ritual purification, the chief fasted from food and spent the night drinking cacina and smoking tobacco to the point of nausea.

*Apalachee woman serving cacina during
a pre-game ritual*

Origins of the Game

The following is Fray Paiva's account of the mythic origins of the game extracted from the native interpreters' notebook:

In long ago days when all the Apalachee were non-Christian there were two chiefs who lived in neighboring villages. One was named Ochuna Nicoguadca, signifying the lightning bolt. The other was Ytonanslac, a wise and elderly man identified with another of the Apalachee's gods. Ytonanslac had an orphaned granddaughter, Nicotaijulo, whose name meant "woman of the sun." The village leaders sent her to fetch water every day. In the course of this employment she became pregnant in some extraordinary way and gave birth to a son whom she hid among some bushes. There, the panther, the bear, and the blue jay found him. They brought the child to his grandfather, Ytonanslac, telling him how his granddaughter, Nicotaijulo, had given birth to the child. Ytonanslac ordered them not to tell anyone else about the child, whom he called Chita.

Ytonanslac reared the child in his house until the age of twelve, at which time his name was changed to Oclafi, meaning "lord of water." In his twentieth year that name was taken from him and he was given the name Eslafiayupi, which had some special meaning the Indians avoided telling the friar by saying they did not know what it meant. From the "lafi" portion of the name, we know it meant lord of something.

As he grew into manhood, Eslafiayupi excelled in courage, in his skill with bow and arrow, and in "chunkey," a game played since the origin of time by all the southeastern tribes.

Because of this renown, he attracted the attention of Ochuna Nicoguadca who thought that he might be the son of Nicotaijulo. This concerned Ochuna particularly because his shamans had foretold that someday a son born to Nicotaijulo was destined to kill him. In order to learn if Eslafiayupi was the man, Ochuna tried to see if he might kill him by presenting three challenges which involved great danger.

Eslafiayupi's grandfather, Ytonanslac, aware of those predictions, told his grandson that before he accepted and acted on any orders or challenges, he should tell him about them. Accordingly, Eslafiayupi did so when Ochuna gave him the first order, which was that he should go to a certain large and very deep sinkhole to obtain raw flint for arrowheads. On being told of this, the grandfather said to him, "Son, this spring is very deep. You cannot obtain the flint from it without risking your life." He then gave Eslafiayupi some special beads made of shell and told him to give the beads to a little bird he would find diving there and ask the bird to get the flint for him. The grandson did so and thus received the flint and brought it to Ochuna Nicoguadca.

Ochuna Nicoguadca then gave his suspected nemesis two more dangerous tasks to perform. Eslafiayupi was to bring canes for arrow shafts from a certain canebrake which was filled with venomous snakes, and some fledgling eagles from a certain treetop nest. When the young rival, aided by the advice of his grandfather, returned successful and unscathed from those two ventures, Ochuna Nicoguadca concluded that he could not kill the young man in this fashion because of special powers that he possessed. He then arranged that they should play the first ball game. This was the origin of the Apalachee game by which its rules and supernatural aspects were established. The loser, apparently, was to forfeit his life.

On the day appointed for the game, Ytonanslac's team entered the plaza of Ochuna Nicoguadca's village. On being asked if their team was at full strength, Ytonanslac's team said no, that they were short so many people. Their rivals told them to choose those needed from some young men from Yto-nanslac's village who were present there. Among them was Eslafiayupi, who gave the appearance of being ill, leaning up against a post, wrapped in a cloak made of feathers. According to the friar's account, upon Eslafiayupi's entering the game, the battle was begun. And when those of Ytonanslac had reached seven, Eslafiayupi let out a thunder-like roar and all were terrified. And Eslafiayupi was recognized to be Nicoguadca, the lightning-flash born of the sun whose name is Nico, and of Nicotaijulo or woman of the sun.

Ever since that first game, it remained an omen that the first team to reach seven points would win because Nicoguadca was on their side. The opposing team always lost heart at that point, making the prophecy self-fulfilling.

The story of the ball game's origin ended thus. When Eslafiayupi-Nicoguadca wished to die, he called together all his leaders to inform them that he was going to die, and told them that whoever wished to become Nicoguadca and remain in his place had to kill seven tascaias (ordinary warriors) and three hitas tascaias (warriors of a higher category). He then instructed his subjects that as soon as he died, they should put his body in some big pots along with squash, melon, and watermelon, and fill them with water so that he might be converted into steam. In this way, he might remember them and return to give them water when they had planted their fields. He said to them, "When you hear it thunder, it is a sign that I am coming." The friar closed the story with the comment "And thus did Nicoguadca go they say and he did what he promised. And up to the present they, and especially the older ones, continue to believe that when it thundered, Eslafiayupi was on his way to give them water."

Among the leaders of the warrior caste there were individual "Great Warriors" as late as the 1670s who identified themselves as reincarnations or representations of the original Eslafiayupi-become-Nicoguadca, or Thunder-god. Paiva noted that his parishoners had identified a leading warrior from the San Luis mission as such a reincarnation of Nicoguadca. This individual, named Talpagana Luis, whom the friar knew from service in the mission earlier in the 1670s, had died before Paiva returned to that post in the mid-1670s for a second time. Parishoners told the friar that at the time of his death, Talpagana Luis told the bystanders that he would have to come back and burn the goal posts. The friar confessed reluctantly, "As though by the just judgments of God Our Lord, a lightning bolt fell that year and burned the post at San Luis. And the next year another fell and burned the one at Bacuqua, and it so happened that two years earlier another one had burned the post at Patale."

The Apalachee ball game was begun by tossing the ball into the air.

Fray Paiva's Description of the Game

The friar's use of the word "battle" to describe the beginning of the game was
well chosen. He noted that all the players bunched together "like a clump of pine
cones," waiting for a village leader to toss the ball in the air to start the game. As
soon as someone caught the ball, a general melee ensued as the rival players
struggled with one another to gain or retain possession of the ball. The following
is the friar's graphic portrait of this mob scene.

*And they fall upon one another at full tilt. And the last to arrive climb up over
their bodies, using them as stairs. And, to enter, others [step on] their faces,
heads, or bellies as they encounter them, taking no notice [of them] and aiming
kicks without any concern whether it is to the face or to the body, while in other
places still others pull at arms or legs with no concern as to whether they may
be dislocated or not while still others have their mouths filled with dirt. When
this pileup begins to become untangled, they are accustomed to find four or five
stretched out like tuna; over there are others gasping for breath because,
inasmuch as some are wont to swallow the ball, they are made to vomit it up by
squeezing their windpipe or by kicks to the stomach. Over there lie others with
an arm or leg broken.*

The violence was not always confined to the playing field. At the
time Paiva composed his tirade against the game in 1676, he
reported that of five successive games at San Luis, "not one
concluded without becoming a live war," which apparently
spread to the spectators. He concluded that only the presence
of Spanish soldiers prevented serious incidents. Among the
injuries produced by the brutality of the game were broken
legs, permanently maimed hands, broken ribs, and loss of
sight in an eye. It was not unknown, he noted, for
people to be killed in the course of a contest,
asserting that he was aware of two such deaths
on the playing field at San Luis.

After the initial outburst, the play
apparently settled down to

something more resembling an organized game. There would be considerable
running back and forth in the heat of the summer afternoons, which was when the
game was played in order to assure adequate rain for the crops. The friar described
the players' faces as ruddy from their exertions, "as if they were aflame," and noted
that buckets of water were used to revive those who became exhausted.

As a consequence of the campaign waged by Fray Paiva, playing of the game was
prohibited in 1676. A renewal of the prohibition the following year suggests that the
initial ban was not successful. Governor Juan Márquez Cabrera, who landed in
Apalachee in the fall of 1680 on his way to assume his post in St. Augustine,
found ball posts still standing and the game still being played in Apalachee
upon his arrival.

*The Apalachee ball game held much religious
and social significance. The ball was about
the size of a golf ball and was made of
hardened clay covered with buckskin.*

CHAPTER 4

Trouble for the Apalachee Missions, 1674-1704

The Christianization of Apalachee was complete by 1672, but beyond that bare statement little else is known about developments in the province between late 1657 and 1674. It was undoubtedly impacted by a 1659 measles epidemic that allegedly killed 10,000 of Spanish Florida's Indians. Governor Rebolledo was deposed in 1658 when the Council of the Indies took the unusual step of recommending his immediate removal and imprisonment for having created a situation that seemed to threaten the total loss of the Florida missions. His plans for expanding the Spanish presence in Apalachee were shelved for a generation because of the Indians' continued opposition to that development. As the 1650s drew to a close, a period of accommodation appears to have begun that was to last into the 1680s. However, it was not the "Golden Age" that some have suggested.

DEMOGRAPHY

Records from 1675 provide the first village-by-village census of the Apalachee missions. Unfortunately, there is good reason to believe that estimates for the individual missions routinely underestimated the population both in Apalachee and elsewhere. The individualized listing indicates a total population of only 7580 for the eleven missions inhabited by Apalachee and 300 for the Chine mission. But the record of confirmations administered by Cuba's bishop a little earlier that year indicates that there were at least 10,000 Apalachee living at the missions. This is borne out by a remark by the bishop about the number of Apalachee women whom he found wearing nothing more than a skirt that covered them from waist to knee. He provided 4081 dresses for the women that were woven of Spanish moss, the same material they used for their skirts. With that caution about the census's reliability, the following is a mid-1675 listing of the Apalachee missions drawn up by the deputy governor, Juan Fernández de Florencia. It gives each mission's population and the distances between missions.

1675 Census of Apalachee Missions

Mission	Population	Location
San Luis	1400	1 league from there to
San Damián de Cupaica	900	2 leagues to
San Antonio de Bacuqua	120	2 leagues to
San Pedro de Patale	500	4 leagues to
San Joseph de Ocuya	900	1.5 leagues to
San Juan de Aspalaga	800	1 league to
San Francisco de Ocone	200	0.5 + league to
Concepción de Ayubale	800	1.5 leagues to
San Lorenzo de Ivitachuco	1200	1.5 leagues to Asile
Candelaria (Tama-Yamasee)	300	1.5 + leagues from San Luis and 2 leagues to
San Martín de Tomole	700	2 + leagues to
Santa Cruz de Ytuchafun	60	
Assumption of Our Lady (Capara, Amacano, and Chine)	300	on the path to the sea from San Luis

Ivitachuco was reputed to have 2600 people in 1655. The figure for 1675 indicates that its population had been almost halved during the interim, giving a probable indication of the impact of epidemics in Apalachee during the intervening two decades.

1689 Census of Apalachee Missions

San Lorenzo de Hivitachuco	1000
Concebción de Ayubale	1250
San Francisco Oconi	400
San Juan de Aspalaga	250
San Joseph de Ocuya	1000
Santa Cruz de Hichutafun	150
San Martín de Tomoli	650
Nra. Señora de la Tama	400
San Pedro de los Chines	150
San Luis de Talimali	1500
San Pedro y S. Pablo de Patali	600
San Antonio de Bacucua	250
San Damián de Yscambi	2000

The evidence for the underestimation of the population on the 1675 listing is supported by a second listing of the population of individual missions from 1689. This list was drawn up by Cuba's bishop, Diego Ebelino de Compostela, based on information he had requested from the priests under his jurisdiction. The bishop listed only the number of families in each mission. But he stipulated that to convert the number of families into the number of individuals, the families should be multiplied by five. The bishop's listing placed a total of 9600 Indians in Apalachee in 1689, exclusive of the Tocobaga. He omitted them because their village was not a mission. The census shown here is the bishop's list converted into the total number of individuals.

Even a hasty comparison of the 1675 and 1689 lists reveals several significant increases and declines in the populations of individual villages. Most spectacular is Cupaica's rise from the alleged 900 in 1675 to 2000 in 1689. Also noteworthy was Ayubale's surge from 800 to 1250. On the downside, Aspalaga's collapse from 800 to 250 is also spectacular. There is no explicit evidence to account for changes of that magnitude. The impact of the underestimates of 1675 is probably represented in San Luis's increase of a mere 100, if one can assume that San Luis had not been affected seriously by any epidemics since 1675. Migration from one mission to another may account for some of Cupaica's increase. Existence of such migration is reflected in a regulation issued by the official visitor in 1695 forbidding the deputy governor to permit any families to pass from villages that were on the royal road to others that were not. Cupaica's known move to a site about a mile or so west of the Ochlockonee River may have made it an attractive destination for such migrations. Bacuqua's location on Apalachee's northwest frontier may account for some of its increase in population. Because of unhappiness with Antonio Matheos, Apalachee's unpopular deputy governor in the mid-1680s, a number of Apalachee migrated to the Creek country along the Chattahoochee River. Some of Aspalaga's loss of population may have been a consequence of troubles in that village. A son of Aspalaga's principal chief was among the Apalachee who came with the Creek forces that attacked Apalachee in 1704.

Compared to the native peoples of Spanish Florida who were missionized earlier, the Apalachee survived in greater numbers until 1704. The same circumstances may have applied to the Apalachee's immediate eastern neighbors, the Yustaga, who also survived in greater numbers than did the remainder of their fellow western Timucua.

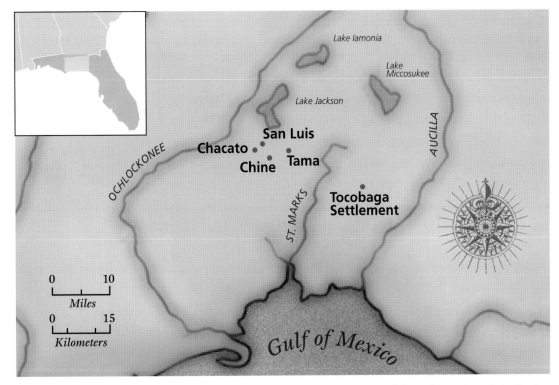

Non-Apalachee settlements in Apalachee Province

Non-Apalachee in the Province

Records from the mid-1670s indicate that a number of non-Apalachee tribes had moved into the province, and most of their villages became mission centers. They were the Tama and Yamasee from central Georgia's Oconee River valley; Chine, Pacara, and Amacano, who probably came from west Florida's coast; Chacato from the Marianna area; and Tocobaga from the north Tampa Bay region. All but the Tocobaga settlement eventually became missions.

Tama and Yamasee were basically the same people and were probably refugees from attacks on their homeland by native peoples from Virginia whom English sources refer to as Westo. When the Chine mission was first established in April 1674, Chine, Pacara, and Amacano, who all spoke the same language, were living together in a village named Chaccabi on a small stream Spaniards called Rio Chachave. It flowed into western Apalachee Bay and was probably today's Spring Creek. These people were probably closely related to the Chacato. A mission settlement was established by Chacato in Apalachee about a mile west of San Luis. The migrants were a remnant from two Chacato missions established slightly earlier in the Marianna region. Unrest at the Chacato missions and their fear of attack by hostile Chisca from the Choctawhatchee River region motivated the Chacato's move into Apalachee territory. Little is known about the reason for the Tocobaga's coming. It probably resulted from the encroachment of their traditional enemies, the Calusa, into Tampa Bay.

THE BEGINNING OF THE END

By the mid-1670s, the encounter phase between Spaniard and Apalachee had ended. The mission system and the Spanish military presence in Apalachee appeared to be solidly rooted, and most natives acquiesced to it. The prospects seemed promising for developing a stable Christian society that would permit Spanish authorities to push the "rim of Christendom" farther west, northwest, and south to embrace the Chacato, the Apalachicola, and the nonagricultural peoples of south Florida. But beginning in the second half of the 1670s, troubles began to appear that would disturb, and later destroy, the routine that had been established.

By contrast with the years 1657 to 1674, the thirty years from 1674 to 1704 represent the best known period of the Apalachee missions, probably, to a considerable degree, because of these growing troubles. As happens today, conflicts and disasters generate far more records than do times of peace and prosperity. In Apalachee, as in Spanish Florida in general, this thirty-year period was preeminently and increasingly one of hostility and unrest that ended in mid-1704 with abandonment of the province by its surviving natives and Spaniards alike.

A variety of factors was responsible, among them England's establishment of Charles Town, South Carolina, in 1670 and the Spaniards' decision during the 1670s to build a massive stone castillo in St. Augustine in response to the British threat. In Apalachee proper, beginning around 1675, Spanish civilian settlement and ranch development led to increased tension. It was exacerbated by a governor's appointment and support of an irascible deputy governor in the mid-1680s who alienated most of Apalachee's native inhabitants. That governor and his successor adopted policies to counter English commercial activity among the Apalachicola and instigated measures in response to rumors of French activity on the Gulf Coast west of Apalachee in the 1680s. These changes resulted in expanded Spanish demands on Apalachee's native inhabitants and created a state of war with the Apalachicola. Finally, there was the outbreak of a general European war at the turn of the century to influence the succession to Spain's throne. The war gave Britain a plausible excuse for open hostilities against the Spaniards in Florida and the natives allied to them in order to seize control of Florida and eliminate natives who might thwart British ambitions of expansion.

The Chisca Raids

The year 1675 provided the first intimations of the troubles to come as news reached Apalachee about traders from Charles Town moving into the hinterland to establish contact with non-Christian natives. The traders were eager to purchase as slaves any Indians the non-Christian Indians might capture. Some of the Indians contacted by the traders were neighbors of the Apalachee and nominal subjects of the Spanish Crown who had traded with the mission centers since the late 1640s. The English demand for Indian slaves encouraged Chisca Indians from west Florida and Yamasee who had migrated to the vicinity of Apalachee to launch the first raids on outlying Apalachee hamlets and farmsteads. They captured women and children to sell as slaves, an activity far more lucrative than trading deerhides.

By early summer of 1677, some of the Indians making the nighttime raids were identified as Chisca from a settlement on the Choctawhatchee River. In September, once the harvest was in, a small force of about 190 warriors drawn largely from San Luis and Cupaica, with a few Chine and Chacato impressed as guides, set out to punish the Chisca. The spirit in which the expedition was conceived is reflected in the native leaders' comments on its genesis.

Apalachee raid against the Chisca

One night the aforesaid leaders Juan Mendoza and Matheo [Chuba], and Bentura, inija, with other leaders of this place of San Luis, happening to be together on alert discussing matters in the council house of San Luis, proposed setting out to search for the enemy. And some were saying we would not be given permission, while others said, no, they would not refuse us this; for we are disturbed daily and have no peace. And they are killing our relatives constantly. And what hurts us most is the ones they carry off as slaves and what they are doing with the young women. For we are Christians and vassals of the King our lord.... And of one mind we all went to seek permission from Captain Juan Fernández [de Florencia] as our Lieutenant and War Captain and leader in this province.... He granted them the permission and cheered and encouraged them and promised to help them with all that he could. And all the commanders and chiefs and the rest of the leaders came back to this council house very happy and jubilant.

The religious spirit that animated the expedition is reflected in the warriors' bringing along the banner of the San Luis cofradía, with a crucifix emblazoned on one side and Our Lady of the Rosary on the other, to serve as a battle standard. As the main contingent charged the enemy's palisaded village, it carried the banner aloft. That spirit is evident as well in the leaders' exhortation to their men at a stop along the way, reminding them that "they were men capable of defending their villages' women and children, and that if God should help them, they would achieve their desire of seeing their enemies [and that] God and His Most Holy Mother would favor them as Christians."

Our Lady of the Rosary. Photo by Helen Sosaya. Reproduced courtesy of the Museum of New Mexico, Neg. No. 123136.

As they were leaving the village of Sauocola, where they crossed the Apalachicola River, its chief, Baltasar, came out to join them with six of his men, remarking that "although he was only a recent Christian, he had his heart in God and in his most holy mother and that with great pleasure he was coming along to die for God our Lord and for his King and for his country."

The warriors followed the native trail westward to just past the abandoned Chacato villages in the Marianna region. To escape detection by Chisca sentries posted farther west on the trail, the Apalachee swung southwestward through the forest to intersect a different trail to the Chisca village that Chacato and Pansacola fishermen living with the Chisca had recently opened. This maneuver enabled the Apalachee to surprise their enemy and kill a considerable number of them during the attack. Only five Apalachee were killed and forty wounded. The attacking Apalachee warriors saw the hand of God at work in the heat of the battle when a tree in the village caught fire from their firearms and its burning leaves set fire to many houses, killing many of the enemy who had sought refuge in them. What struck them most about this event was that although the tree was green, "its leaves should burn as though they were tinder." They reported that "on seeing this miracle, the Chiscas, inasmuch as the river forms a gorge there, threw themselves into it, women with children at the breast as well as men. And although we wished to catch them and bring them back alive, they were already almost dead and drowned." After remaining at the village for several days to prepare the severely wounded for the long trek back to Apalachee, the victors set fire to the rest of the village and headed home.

The Apalachee leaders' account of this campaign was taken down in the Apalachee tongue by Juan Fernández de Florencia. It illustrates the difficulties that the Indians had in waging war over a great distance with forces of any size beyond that of a small raiding party that could live off the land.

Labor Grievances

From the time Spanish authorities forced the Apalachee to accept the labor draft in exchange for the amnesty that they granted to most of the Indians involved in the 1647 revolt, the demand for labor became a constant irritant for the natives. When Apalachee's leaders agreed to that demand, they considered it a temporary measure in reparation for the destruction of life and property resulting from the revolt. But Spaniards considered it a permanent, ongoing obligation once it had been introduced and accepted. Around 1675, tensions rose dramatically as the demand for native labor increased in response to the construction of the new stone fort in St. Augustine, the expansion of the San Luis garrison, and the establishment of Spanish ranches and farms in Apalachee.

In 1676, Fray Alonso Moral, then a thirty-three-year veteran of the Florida missions, presented a revealing portrait of the evils associated with this labor system.

> *All the natives of those provinces suffer great servitude, injuries, and vexations from the fact that the governors, deputy governors, and soldiers oblige them to carry loads on their shoulders to the province of Apalachee and to other areas and also to bring loads from those regions to the fort of St. Augustine. And it usually happens that to enhance their own interests they pretend that this labor is in Your Majesty's service, without paying them what is just for such intolerable work. And if they give them something now and again, it is a hoe or an axe or a cheap blanket or some other thing of such slight value to pay for their work, which involves carrying a cargo on their shoulders from the fort to the province of Apalachee, which is eighty leagues distant and the same to return. ... And in addition to this, in order to employ them further, they detained them in St. Augustine for as long as they wish ... with very short rations, such as giving them only two pounds of corn a day and giving them for pay one real a day at the most. This sum is usually given them in the form of old rubbish of little or no value or utility to them.*

Demands for Apalachee labor to build forts was a major grievance.

The friar went on to observe that 300 Apalachee men were recruited each year for work in St. Augustine during the planting season, when they were most needed at home.

The intensity of the natives' resentment over these labor demands is reflected in a friar's comment about the Apalachicola Indians' quick rejection of a mission attempt in their land in 1679. The friar linked the rejection to the tie between Christianization and the labor obligation. He maintained that the Apalachicola's paramount chief would drop his opposition to the mission's presence if he were assured that his people would not be subjected to the same labor demands that were being made on the Apalachee. Although his argument probably represented wishful thinking, it definitely indicates the unpopularity of the labor draft.

Establishment of Spanish Ranches

Pablo de Hita Salazar, a new governor installed in mid-1675, commissioned Fernández de Florencia to resurrect the plans for a Spanish settlement in Apalachee Province. These plans had remained dormant since the killing of Deputy Governor Claudio Luis in 1647 and the Crown's abrupt removal of Governor Rebolledo in 1658. Upon the outbreak of trouble among the recently missionized Chacato a few weeks after Hita Salazar's installation, the governor expressed concern about the firearms and ammunition that many Apalachee were acquiring from their trade with ships from Havana. He suggested to the Crown that it was time to reactivate Rebolledo's plans to build a genuine fort in Apalachee. He explained that the unrest among the Chacato provided a good pretext for the Spanish authorities to conceal

Study by Edward Jonas. Reproduced courtesy of the artist.

their real motives for building the fort and promoting Spanish settlement and to overcome the expected Apalachee resistance to the plans.

Since the fort was not actually constructed until a few years before abandonment of the province, it did not become a major source of trouble. But development of Spanish ranching and the Spanish settlement associated with it progressed rapidly, bringing with it resentment and discontent that seriously alienated the natives. This development ultimately contributed substantially to the destruction of the missions and Spanish loss of the province and its people.

It is not known whether Apalachee leaders objected to the establishment of
Spanish ranches from the outset. A Crown decree issued early in the 1680s forbidding chiefs, as well as governors, to make land grants suggests that some native
leaders were involved in the process.

The expanded Spanish presence in the province arising from the introduction
of ranching by Spaniards and enlargement of the San Luis garrison escalated the
injustices that the natives suffered at the hands of the Spaniards. Juana Cathalina
de Florencia became infamous for her mistreatment of various Apalachee and her
demands for unpaid labor from them. She required the village of San Luis to furnish
her with six women each day to grind maize without pay, another Indian to bring in
a pitcher of milk daily from the country, and other such services. She slapped the
face of a hapless chief who failed once to bring her the fish she expected every
Friday. In another instance her demand for labor and carelessness resulted in the
drowning of a retarded Indian child who was still nursing and crawling at the age
of five. The incident arose when Juana Cathalina summoned a group of native
women to gather chestnuts for her. When the retarded child's mother objected,
since the child needed constant supervision, Juana promised to care for it. When the
mother returned around six o'clock, the child was nowhere to be seen. The child
had drowned when it crawled or rolled down the hill on which Juana Cathalina's
house was located and fell into a pond or spring.

In April 1699, Ivitachuco's chief appealed to a Spanish friend in St. Augustine
to write to the king. The chief was seeking a remedy for abuses still being inflicted
on the Apalachee by members of the Florencia clan, despite his repeated complaints
to the Spanish authorities in Florida. He reported that the deputy governor, Jacinto
Roque Pérez, was allowing Francisco Florencia and Joseph Salinas to force young
men to work on their haciendas without receiving any religious instruction or
having the opportunity to hear Mass. He also complained that they were keeping
women on their haciendas in violation of explicit orders by the official visitor.
The chief observed that Roque Pérez had dismissed those orders as not amounting
to anything and remarked that it was his will that would prevail. The chief also
reported that many Apalachee were fleeing their villages, some to the woods and
others to Charles Town, to escape the amount of work imposed on them by the
Florencias without any compensation. Subsequently, the chief made a last appeal
to the king for the abolition of the labor draft but to no avail.

Another chronic grievance caused by the presence of Spanish ranches was damage done to the natives' crops by the free-ranging cattle from haciendas that were much closer to native villages than Spanish law permitted. In response to such complaints, the visitor Joaquín de Florencia required Marcos Delgado and Diego Jiménez (who was married to a Florencia) to move their haciendas, but he did nothing about the other ranches in contention, including those belonging to Juan Fernández de Florencia and Francisco and Diego de Florencia. The chiefs of San Luis and Ivitachuco complained to the king in February 1699 about the continuation of this problem. They argued that, because the Florencias were so powerful, justice was not being rendered to the Apalachee.

An additional source of unrest that followed the introduction of ranching and farming by Spanish settlers was the newcomers' forceful and rapid economic monopoly over exports. Prior to Spanish involvement, the Apalachee had dominated the sale of the province's produce to St. Augustine and Havana. In 1700, St. Augustine's pastor, Alonso de Leturiondo, remarked that in the period before 1670, stimulated by Spanish demand for their produce, the Indians had greatly increased their stock-raising, planting, and hunting and gathering to supply bacon, lard, nuts, and other goods for export. However, once a number of Spanish families acquired land in Apalachee, they sought to corner the market on such produce, especially that for hogs and their by-products, in order to raise the selling price artificially. Consequently, they began to raise hogs and to buy those raised by the Indians. When necessary, they used violence or other pressure to secure their objectives. Spaniards took advantage of the Indians' understandable reticence in dealing with them and their fear of the consequences if they crossed someone who was well connected, such as one of the Florencias. At times, the Indians were forced to sell their produce at prices even lower than they had charged when they controlled the market or to hand goods over in exchange for nothing more than a promise to pay. The secretary or notary for Juan de Ayala Escobar's 1701 visitation of the province learned that such Spanish traders' taking of horses and hogs from the Indians without paying for them had caused an accumulation of more than 3000 pesos in unpaid debt. The secretary's findings provide an explanation for the radical remedy Alonso de Leturiondo had suggested a year earlier as the only real solution to the Spanish settlers' mistreatment of the Indians. He recommended the expulsion of all Spanish

Oxcarts were first introduced into Apalachee Province in the 1680s.

settlers from Apalachee and a prohibition to prevent the soldiers stationed there from engaging in any farming or commerce. Leturiondo suggested that this enterprise be left to the Indians as it had been prior to the 1670s.

The notary for Ayala y Escobar's 1701 visitation, Manuel de Quiñones, realized that, because of the visitor's ties to the Florencia faction, the Apalachee feared to speak their minds to him. The natives had learned from experience that such an exercise would be futile and would result only in retribution from the Florencias once the visitor had left. After becoming aware that the province was a tinderbox, and that only the influence of Ivitachuco's chief had prevented a revolt to eliminate the Spaniards from Apalachee, Quiñones conducted a visitation session of his own. It was held in an isolated building somewhere in the middle of the sprawling settlement of San Luis away from the center of the Spanish settlement. Indians from all over the province attended. Apalachee guards were posted outside to prevent any resident Spaniards from eavesdropping on the Indians' testimony. The session began in the evening and lasted until two o'clock in the morning. He recorded seventy-two pages of complaints, revealing the Spaniards' whipping of Indian women to the point of causing those who were pregnant to miscarry, their taking of Indian women for their own sexual gratification, and Juana Cathalina's responsibility for the drowning of the Indian child left in her care, to mention a few.

When Ayala y Escobar learned of Quiñones's session, he demanded a copy of the record to show to Roque Pérez and the Florencias. Quiñones refused and did not give it to him until the closing of the visitation at Salamototo, the mission located where the St. Johns River crossed the Spanish trail. It is not clear whether Ayala y Escobar gave Governor Joseph de Zúñiga y Zerda the entire record, which would have revealed the banality and ineffectiveness of his visitation. The governor was concerned enough with what he saw to dispatch Bernardo Nieto Caravajal to Apalachee to pacify the Indians, but he apparently gave him only two or three sheets of the record Quiñones had compiled. Nieto Caravajal proved to be a venal individual. After being showered with gifts by Apalachee's Spanish families, he did nothing to requite the Indians' grievances. Governor Zúñiga y Zerda apparently did nothing further to investigate or remedy the grievances that inspired the complaints.

We know of Quiñones's efforts in 1701 to secure a redressing of the Indians' grievances only because the matter continued to disturb him many years later. In 1719, on the arrival of a new governor, Antonio de Benavides, Quiñones presented him with a manifesto. It described the earlier Spanish officials' responsibility, along with that of Spanish residents of Apalachee, for the loss of the province in 1704 because of the miscarriages of justice that thoroughly alienated most of the natives. In a formal inquiry to corroborate Quiñones's charges, the governor questioned soldiers who had served in Florida in that earlier period. They agreed with Quiñones that Apalachee had indeed been lost because of the failure of a succession of official visitors, such as Ayala y Escobar and Caravajal, to remedy the chronic mistreatment of the Indians by Spaniards residing in Apalachee, particularly by Jacinto Roque Pérez and the Florencias. Several of them testified to having seen Nieto Caravajal return from Apalachee accompanied by several packhorses loaded with the gifts of ham, beef, and lard he had received from the Spanish residents there.

Such a belated inquiry into this matter was not as untimely as it might seem, for Benavides had taken over the governorship from the same Juan de Ayala y Escobar of the 1698 and 1701 visitations. He had assumed the office on an interim basis in 1716 on the death of the proprietary governor, Pedro de Olivera y Fullana. Quiñones probably presented his manifesto so that it might become part of the residencia for Ayala y Escobar.

In his manifesto Quiñones revealed that he had been alerted to the Indians' roiling anger in 1701 by an Apalachee cacica who was the wife of a Mexican named Juan Salinas. She warned that all of the Indians of the province were "with a bad heart" toward the Spaniards. She revealed that almost all the Apalachee leaders had decided to revolt and kill all the Spaniards in Apalachee, men, women, and children, but were restrained from doing so by don Patricio Hinachuba, "the head chief and lord of the province."

The Crisis of the Mid-1680s

The province appears to have been almost equally disturbed in the mid-1680s by the antics of its deputy governor, Antonio Matheos, and the refusal of the governor who appointed him, Juan Márquez Cabrera, to remove him as the Apalachee leaders at San Luis requested. Many of the incidents recorded about Matheos's conduct involved interpersonal relations and arbitrary brutality rather than abuses of the sort perpetrated by the Spanish ranchers. Matheos was prone to insulting Indian leaders by addressing them as rogues, liars, cuckolds, dogs, and horses and by disparaging native customs and mores. When he became angry, he struck chiefs and ordinary Indians alike about the head with a club he was accustomed to carry. He was particularly critical of the Apalachee's matrilineal inheritance pattern and their failure to respond to adultery with violence against the wife and her lover. Many of the incidents recorded involved San Luis's rulers, Matheo Chuba and the inija Bip Bentura, and the parish interpreter, Juan Mendoza.

The sheer volume of complaints eventually forced the governor to appoint an agent to look into them. However, the governor severely circumscribed the scope of the inquiry. It was designed for damage control rather than to remedy the grievances and to protect him from the charge of having done nothing. The situation compelled a number of Apalachee to seek refuge among the Apalachicola rather than endure the insults and beatings that Matheos administered so freely.

Abusive behavior by a few of the friars also contributed to alienation and unrest, particularly during the 1680s. The abuses involved frequent use of whipping to discipline Indians, ruffian-like physical violence against chiefs and ordinary parishoners, and excessive demands for labor and tribute. Such friars used whipping to drum Christian mores into the natives or to punish women who failed to meet excessive quotas for hickory-nut oil (for the sanctuary lamps) or for the nuts from which the oil was pressed. Friars had natives whipped for offenses as trivial as missing Mass, even when the natives had seemingly acceptable excuses. Ivitachuco's Fray Bartolomé de Ayala assaulted the paramount early in the 1680s when the chief supplied only 200 of the 300 measures of maize the friar demanded to feed carpenters who were adding a bell tower to the mission's church. Factional disputes within Florida's Franciscan community stalled application of a remedy on the local level. The Franciscan official at Madrid who oversaw the New World friars strongly criticized the Franciscan authorities in Florida, but his death shortly thereafter delayed an effective response. And the friars' exemption from civil justice meant that they could be punished only by church authorities.

Ameliorative Influences

To a degree the Apalachee's alienation was lessened by the sympathy with their plight shown by some of the soldiers. Bip Bentura himself testified that after Matheos injured his head by beating him with a walnut cudgel, soldiers treated his wounds. On another occasion Matheos ordered Bip Bentura to bring him some maize seed for planting a community field. When Bip replied that he had no seed to supply except what he needed for his own family, Matheos sent three soldiers to confiscate it. When the soldiers saw how little maize he had, they left it, saying that they would tell Matheos that they had not found any.

Not long after his abortive inquiry, Governor Márquez Cabrera, at odds with all of Florida's priests, the two treasury officials, and many of St. Augustine's leading Spanish inhabitants, left the city on an unauthorized trip to Cuba. In effect, he temporarily abandoned his responsibilities. His departure led to the reopening of the investigation into Matheos's conduct and his removal under the absent governor's interim successor. On the governor's return, he was imprisoned and shipped to Spain.

The next proprietary governor, Diego de Quiroga y Losada, who arrived early in 1688, made a special effort to placate the aggrieved Apalachee, persuading most of the émigrés to return to their villages. But one Apalachee woman, named Qua, remained among the Apalachicola and became a wife of "Emperor Brims," the paramount chief of Coweta. She became a strong supporter of Coweta's advocacy of an Apalachicola alliance with the English of Charles Town. Another émigré, related to San Luis's chiefly family, married an English trader who came to the Apalachicola country in 1686.

One of the outcomes of the new governor's efforts at conciliation was a letter from the Apalachee chiefs addressed to the king. It was written at the governor's behest in their own language. It is the only document in Apalachee that has been found to date. The friar who translated it into Spanish rendered it "just as it is and sounds," as he phrased it, noting that he "could have touched up its unpolished manner of chatting with our King and Lord" but decided not to change the style.

Translation of the Letter Written by the Apalachee Chiefs to the King

To Charles the Second, our noble holahta, our great King (pin Rey chuba).

God, making us created with his power from wretchedness and nothingness, we are living because of its being his will, although with troubles and misfortunes. It does not matter that, even though we are living thus all the days without ending with our scant understanding, accordingly we say our creator wants it thus. Accordingly, we glorify him and revere him, putting this aside. Also all we nobles and also everyone in common, the old men as well as the old women (who tremble from old age) down to the orphaned and helpless young ones, all those whom we encounter in this territory that is named for the Apalachee tribe (Abalachi tafun), every day and regularly we say: it appears that we do not pay reverence to or respect our great chief (pin holahta chuba) our King. It seems that we do not embrace or receive his noble word with a heart. And on saying this among ourselves, we become more devoted and more obedient and humble to receive your word and commandments as soon as they enter through our ears, as we are doing at present. We could have written them a long time ago because of the obedience that we give them. But the day must not have arrived on which we should have done it. And today it must have arrived. And consequently we do so, revering and smelling the noble soles of your great feet (hachia pulaqui chuba—oliendo buestras nobles plantas). And likewise making you aware of what we are living through and suffering, it being thus for us also and for all those who are in this world, having proceeded from and been created from nothingness by the wish and will of God. It is our priests, the fathers of our souls, whose task it is to clean them, to sweep them out, to absolve them, to give them sight, teaching them the good things, removing us and separating us from the evil ones and ugly ones, leaving us only the ones that are good Christian ones, because you have given them to us for this, having compassion on us. And consequently we are recognizing it and we are believing it with a heart.

The second one. Although we are ignorant persons and although it is so, we make thought with our heart, that the soul belongs to our creator, God, and our body and the government of it, this belongs to our head, which you are, whom we recognize as our great chief (pin holahta chuba) and our noble King (pin Rey pulaqui) as the one to whom it belongs to correct it, instruct it, and punish it. And that just as the plants eat, live, and sustain themselves from the dew that comes with the night. And so we and all these your wretched vassals are maintained and live with your noble and great word. And although we do not see them bodily with our eyes, we see the one who occupies your place, that is to say (your lieutenant), who is the one whom they call governor (governadori) and captain general (capitan general). And we look to this one as to the one who is in your place. And we hear and understand and cherish and keep his word as your very own word, believing it and obeying it. And with this being so, we do thus. And the governors that you give us and send us, some are wise and others do not have wisdom. There are some who like us and esteem us and others who treat us badly. And consequently you should hear us with compassion.

The governor who just finished, who is called Don Juan Marques Cabrera, both for us and for our vassals also (as we are all yours), he has kept everyone very much troubled because we have not had a day in which we saw good work in ourselves or in benefit to our villages or in its vigor or safe-keeping. Nor have we seen a good word, rather only such as was calculated to chill our hearts. And even though it has been like this, we have had patience. There is only one thing in particular that has terrified and saddened our hearts. And accordingly you will hear us out on this very [thing], it being so. That our priests fathers, it being so that they are the ones who teach us all the good things. They also tell us and teach us that the word of God never ends or stops, but that it always keeps traveling on ahead. And this there, like all the things pertaining to faith, we believe it with a heart and we say that thus we understand it, and contemplating thus that the word of God does not stop but rather passes on forward.

And we used to visit the heathens who were living near to our villages and they visited us, welcoming each other and giving each other something to eat, buying some things and selling others of what we had. And accordingly we had them in mind with the thought that we were making in our hearts concerning that the word of God should pass to them and that we would all be Christians and sons of God. While we were living and thinking on this, Don Juan Marques Cabrera, when he was governing fell out with them in a fearful way and made them flee and abandon or leave their settlements. But as soon as this governor came, whom you have now given to us, who is called Don Diego de Quiroga, as soon as he learned about this, as he is a man of good heart and of great understanding, as soon as he arrived in St. Augustine town (tafun) and heard it and under-stood it, he sent to call them with such good words and reasonings that he sent them in order to console their hearts, that they were consoled. On their coming at his call, he has spoken to them, regaled them with clothing and other things. From this they and their hearts have become content and we are [as well]. And we say that God will teach them the truth so that we may all be Christians and serve him. And likewise those of Carlos, who have never been seen [before now] in places of Christians. After having been called by the same Governor Don Diego de Quiroga, the son of the chief came, who is the heir and prince (vsinhulu pulaqui holahta) of that territory. He brought three nobles and counsellors (regidores) at his side and also fifteen warriors or braves who accompanied him. And all were seen in Ivitachucu town (tafun). And he welcomed them all with words of his good understanding and he regaled them with clothes and other things. We know that they returned to their lands from this very content. And all of us are [very content] with this.

Likewise he went to the place and village of

Basisa [where the Tocobaga lived]. And after speaking to them with good words so that they might become Christians, they replied yes. And thus we understood it. From this our hearts are content. He also loves and esteems us so much that it is beyond measure. And he has clothed us. And thus we are letting him know it how also that this year of eighty-eight around the moon of January and its days, he has come to these places and territories that are called Abalachi town, where he has seen us, scrutinized us and thus he has strengthened us in the law of God and things pertaining to faith with sweet words from his good heart. How also in what he does for your noble service and to fulfill or keep your noble word and good direction or governing of our villages. And it being thus and because he says that you ordered and charged it, he went with your command to the port of water, which is where they call San Marcos. And he saw it and recognized that it did not have a fort (castillo) or anything else into which to place us and to defend us from the English or other enemies. And on speaking words of feeling from his heart, he said to us and proposed that that was not good thus. That it would be very good to build a fort or a tower so that if the enemy should come by way of that area, both the soldiers and we could enter there and we would defend ourselves. That on having this, we would be able to live with less fear.

Likewise it will be good that we should build a blockhouse also in this San Luis town for our defense. That he will aid us with iron tools and everything necessary. On our making this reasoning and on our thinking with our hearts, it was the truth and what was useful and beneficial for our villages, we the chiefs and governors of this territory and its villages agreed on an opinion that it should be done as he left it ordered to us. That our hearts are very content and pleased. With this being so, we are praising and giving thanks to our Great God and Father of mercy. And we ask that he may give many days of life to our great chief our King (Pin holahta chuba pin Rey). And we beg of you with devoted hearts around your noble feet that, because of this holahta Governor Don Diego de Quiroga's being a man of such a good heart and of such great understanding, you may have compassion on him and on us. And if the moons and years conform themselves may you set a distant period as the measure for which he may govern us and may you increase them. You will pardon us as our father and principal chief if our words are not good. This arrived up to here. Look at it and understand it. And God go with you. Done in San Luis town of Abalachi by all its holahtas in the year of sixteen hundred and eighty-eight in the moon (hitoc) that is called January on its twenty-first day (nihtaga) etc. Your children who revere and tread upon (guelen) your noble feet.

D. natheu chu ba   holahta juᵒ Mendoza
Dⁿ. Bʳᵃ ybita chuco holahta
Don Alonso pastrana cazique de Petali
bon patricio casiqui be santa cruz
b ygnacio casique de Talpatqui

The Apalachee's contentment with Governor Quiroga y Losada probably was short lived. Apalachee workers cut lumber for a new blockhouse, but it was allowed to rot rather than be used. Instead of devoting time to the fortification, the new governor focused his energy on intrusions into Apalachicola territory that further worsened Apalachee's relations with its people. However, we have no record of Apalachee's leaders having protested Governor Quiroga's policies.

OTHER EUROPEAN INCURSIONS INTO THE SOUTHEAST

The Apalachicola Problem

During Matheos's rule, demands he made in order to deal with English and French intrusions into the lower Southeast further exacerbated his relations with Apalachee's natives. English traders from Charles Town first appeared in the Chattahoochee River Apalachicola villages in 1685. Between September 1685 and Matheos's removal in the spring of 1687, he led three expeditions to the vicinity of Columbus, Georgia, in futile attempts to capture the initial five traders and their successors. One of the traders was Dr. Henry Woodward, who earlier had learned to speak several of the southeastern Indians' languages. Large contingents of Apalachee warriors and a few Yamasee constituted the major part of Matheos's forces on these expeditions. The Apalachee had to provide much of the provisions for these expeditions. Angered by the Apalachicolas' lack of cooperation in handing over the traders or supplying information that would enable the Hispano-Apalachee force to capture them, Matheos wanted to burn a number of the villages. He was dissuaded from doing so on the first expedition by Ivitachuco's chief and other Apalachee leaders, as well as by one of the soldiers who accompanied him. The Apalachee leaders warned him that such drastic action would lead to a complete break with the Apalachicola and inevitably to their attacking Apalachee settlements. During Matheos's second expedition he did burn the four northernmost villages of Coweta, Kasihta, Colomme, and Tasquique because their leaders refused to meet with him or to promise to have no further dealings with the English traders.

The next governor sponsored two more futile expeditions. Finally, in late 1689, he sent Spanish soldiers and Apalachee warriors and carpenters to build a fort on the Chattahoochee River. A permanent presence there would permit a rapid response to the appearance of any English traders. A number of Apalachicola villages moved east to the Ocmulgee and Oconee rivers, negating the Spaniards' efforts. The fort was dismantled and abandoned a little over a year later on orders from the Crown, which disapproved of the governor's action because he had not gotten prior authorization for such an expenditure.

The Search for the La Salle Settlement

Despite Apalachee's remoteness from La Salle's settlement in Texas, its residents were involved in a number of ways in the search for it during Matheos's watch. On orders from Governor Márquez Cabrera, Apalachee carpenters worked on a galliot, or boat, that the governor intended to launch to search for the Mississippi River, where the settlement was believed to be. An overland expedition from Apalachee journeyed in 1686 as far as the Montgomery, Alabama, region before turning back. The first maritime expedition launched by Mexico's viceroy left St. Marks early in 1686 after picking up Chine pilots in Apalachee who were familiar with the Gulf Coast as far west as Mobile. The second vice-regal expedition, sailing from west to east, arrived at St. Marks in the spring of 1687 as an inquiry to scuttle the galliot-building project was ending. The second expedition brought an Apalachee seaman it had rescued; he had been part of a Spanish privateer's search for the La Salle expedition. That search occurred long before Spanish authorities were aware of La Salle's settlement. The privateer's captain had learned of the La Salle expedition and its destination while La Salle was still in Haiti. He sailed to the Gulf Coast in hopes of capturing one of La Salle's ships as a prize. The privateer shipwrecked on the coast, and only the Apalachee seaman and a Mexican boy survived the crew's encounter with hostile Indians identified as Arues.

The Pensacola Bay Exploration of 1693

San Luis and St. Marks were the launching points in 1693 of twin maritime and overland expeditions to explore Pensacola Bay. Apalachee provided foodstuffs, horses, and manpower for those expeditions. The expedition's leader, the newly arrived Governor Laureano de Torres y Ayala, brought maize from Mexico that was ground in the Apalachee missions. Upon the founding of the Pensacola settlement five years later, Apalachee provided laborers to build Pensacola's forts and other structures. It also supplied cowboys to drive Apalachee cattle overland as provisions for the fledgling settlement.

The End in Sight

The Spaniards' preoccupation with the international contests being played out in the Southeast precluded concern for the natives on whose backs their power struggles depended. The many demands and abuses that the Apalachee endured, some of which had been festering since the 1670s and 1680s, only grew at the end of the century. The increased threat of Anglo-Creek attacks provided the impetus to finally begin construction of the blockhouse at San Luis in the mid-1690s. San Luis's native residents cut extra lumber for the blockhouse with the intention of replacing the mission church's thatch roof with a wooden one. But before the Apalachee had a chance to replace the roof, Roque Pérez commandeered the surplus lumber and forced the natives to use it to build houses for one of his brother-in-laws and for other Spanish settlers. To make matters worse, Indians living in the vicinity of the village's center were forced from their houses to make way for the new Spanish homes. Other natives living nearby fled to escape the continual demands for labor on Roque Pérez's own house. Early in 1699 the chiefs of Ivitachuco and San Luis complained to the king that San Luis's native residents were living withdrawn in the woods about two and one-half miles from the village center. They no longer even attended Mass on Sundays because of the hardships imposed on them by the Spanish community at San Luis.

When Colonel James Moore and his Indian allies arrived in the beginning of 1704, many of the Apalachee went over to the invading forces or put up only a half-hearted resistance. The Spaniards' loss of Apalachee constituted more of a collapse than a conquest.

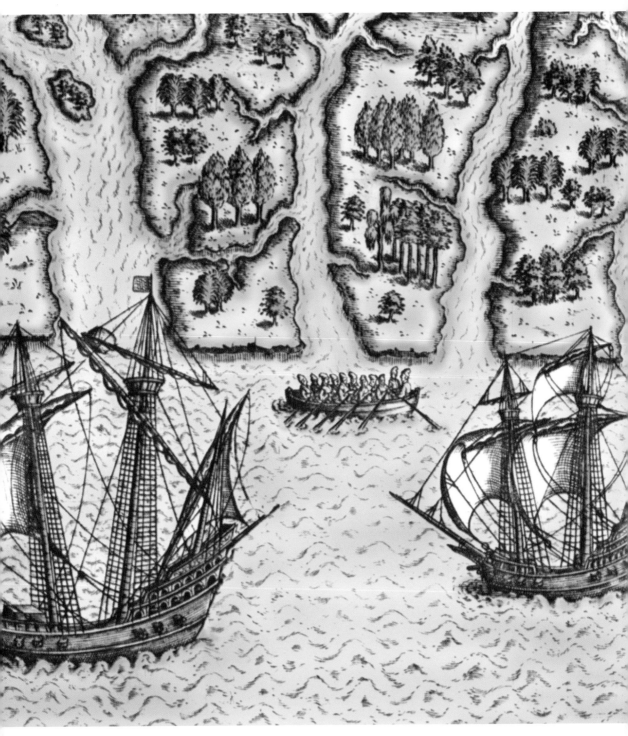

*A number of maritime expeditions were
launched from Apalachee Bay.*

CHAPTER 5

The End of the Missions

The first move toward the final destruction of the hinterland Florida missions occurred at dawn on May 20, 1702. An Apalachicola force that had left Achito made a surprise attack on the Timucua mission of Santa Fé, burning much of the village, including its church. Western Timucua's deputy governor, who was based there, rallied his forces behind a stockade that served as a fence for the friary's garden. They stopped the attackers' advance, and the invaders withdrew after a three-hour battle. A little later the deputy governor set out in pursuit with inadequate forces, unaware that the enemies' numbers had been augmented after the battle. His small Spanish and Timucua force overtook the enemy after traveling about fifteen miles, blundering into the center of a crescent-shaped formation the enemy had established to ambush them. They were trapped as the crescent closed on them.

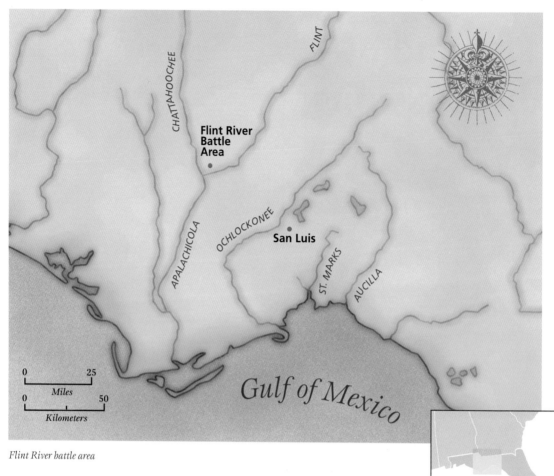

Flint River battle area

That disaster set the stage for the first act in the drama of Apalachee's destruc-
tion, which was played out in mid-October of that year on the banks of the Flint
River. Some of Apalachee's leaders, fearful that more such attacks would follow if
Christians did not avenge the attack on Santa Fé, pressed Spanish authorities to
permit a reprisal. The Apalachee's fears, based on first-hand knowledge of their
Indian neighbors' war practices, were indeed justified. In the days prior to the
encounter on the Flint River, the Apalachicola and other natives allied with the
British met at Achito and targeted Apalachee's Bacuqua and Cupaica missions.
While the Apalachicola were planning this attack, Apalachee traitors forewarned
them of the planned Apalachee reprisal. With that knowledge, they prepared an
ambush for the Apalachee along the trail at the crossing of the Flint. The largely

Apalachee force of 800 warriors, who included some Timucua and Chacato, suffered a disastrous rout. Many of the 300 or so who escaped left their arms behind. The defeat and demoralization brought about by this battle facilitated the destruction of Apalachee, which began early in 1704.

The planned attack on St. Augustine by South Carolina Governor James Moore was among the topics discussed by the native leaders assembled at Achito in October 1702. A Christian Chacato woman living there learned of this plan and hurried to Apalachee to alert Spanish authorities. She reached San Luis during the afternoon of October 21, 1702, just after the disaster on the Flint. Her message reached St. Augustine on October 27, enabling the governor to warn his forces, but he does not seem to have warned his northern coastal outposts on Amelia Island or at the San Pedro sentinel post.

THE ANGLO-CREEK ATTACK ON APALACHEE

Between January and August 1704, Apalachee lost its entire native population and its Spanish community, along with the thriving ranching and farming operations of both groups. Moore, the former governor, began his invasion of Apalachee in January 1704 with an attack on the mission village of Ayubale. His choice of it as his first target probably was not an accident but rather a concession to his native allies in reprisal for the murder of the Tasquique traders five years earlier by

Francisco de Florencia and his Chacato cohorts. When Moore captured Deputy Governor Captain Juan Ruiz de Mejía and some Spanish soldiers, he offered to release them to the Spaniards remaining at San Luis in exchange for Apalachee's Chacato population.

The native inhabitants of Ayubale, encouraged by their friar, stoutly resisted the invasion by defending the church

compound until they exhausted their ammunition and the attackers set fire to the church, forcing their surrender. When the deputy governor learned of the attack on Ayubale, he set out with most of his soldiers and the loyal warriors he was able to assemble to go to Ayubale's relief. Captain Jacinto Roque Pérez was left in charge of San Luis's fort with very few soldiers. The Hispano-Apalachee force encountered the attackers on the road to Ayubale and were eventually routed when their ammunition ran low and the deputy governor was wounded. He and a number of soldiers and Indians were captured. After this second battle, two of the soldiers and possibly more than forty of the captured Apalachee were burned at the stake in retaliation for the fatalities that the native invaders had suffered.

Moore and his forces made no further attacks on the missions at the time. He was aware of the discontent among many of the Apalachee over their treatment by the Spanish residents and of the terror he had induced in them by the torture inflicted on prisoners taken during the second battle. He offered freedom to the inhabitants of all the rest of the missions on the condition that they would agree to leave the province with his forces. A considerable number of warriors had already joined his party when it first arrived in the province. An additional 1300 Apalachee from several missions accepted Moore's terms. Ivitachuco's chief remained loyal to Spain but purchased immunity from attack by agreeing to hand over his church's silver and some provisions.

To contact the Spaniards at San Luis, Moore used Fray Angel Miranda as his negotiator. Moore did nothing more than to attempt to extract a ransom for the wounded deputy governor and some of his soldier prisoners. His ransom demands included having the Spaniards hand over the Chacato and money. Moore threatened to kill everyone at the fort if his demand for the Chacato was rejected. To his credit, Roque Pérez twice rejected that demand, informing Moore that it was out of the question because the Chacato were subjects of Spain's king. Roque Pérez did so despite the fact that his brother-in-law, Diego Jiménez, was one of the captured soldiers who was to remain imprisoned at Charles Town for about five years. In his demand for money, Moore asked for a ransom of 400 pesos. Roque Pérez agreed to feed him that ransom out of the mouths of his cannon if he would come to San Luis to receive it.

The people of seven missions survived and remained in Spanish territory when Moore left the province: San Luis, Ivitachuco, Cupaica, Patale, Aspalaga, the

The abandonment of San Luis

Chacato, and the people of an unidentified town who fled into Timucua territory accompanied by their friar. The Spanish governor identified those carried off by Moore's forces as being from Ayubale, Tomole, Capole, Tama, and Ocatoses (the last were identified elsewhere as Tawasa). Since most if not all of the enslaved natives were from Ayubale, his claim that he had captured more than 4000 natives clearly appears to be unfounded. The surviving missions of San Luis, Ivitachuco, and Cupaica were three of the province's four largest missions. Although Ayubale was the fourth, the remaining villages did not have enough people to account for that many slaves, as well as the 1300 natives from Apalachee who accompanied Moore while remaining free.

In a second attack in June–July 1704, a Creek force dealt a death blow to the province. The invaders captured the inhabitants of Patale and Aspalaga. Although they occupied and destroyed Cupaica, most of its people had taken refuge at San Luis on orders of the deputy governor. An enemy force swept around to the south of San Luis and captured seven Spaniards who were coming up from St. Marks on El Camino Real, or the royal road. When that force withdrew, only San Luis, Ivitachuco, and the Chacato remained. The native inhabitants of San Luis, who now included those from Cupaica, told the Spaniards that they were weary of Spanish promises of aid and reinforcements that never arrived, saying that if they left the province, they would not go to a Spanish-controlled area. They also noted that if they decided to remain, it would be to join the enemy in their attack on the Spaniards in the blockhouse. Some Spanish soldiers were sympathetic to the Apalachee in that they too were promised reinforcements that never came.

In view of reports that a third enemy attack was in the offing, the governor and his council authorized abandonment of the province. The native leaders at San Luis led a caravan of about 800 natives on a westward overland trek. They included most of the remaining people native to San Luis, part of Cupaica's population, the Christian Chacato of Apalachee, and a few non-Christians from a refugee Yamasee

village. The natives drove their remaining cattle before them heading toward Pensacola, with Mobile the ultimate destination for most of them. A Frenchman from Mobile accompanied them. He had brought an invitation from Jean Baptiste Le Moyne de Bienville to settle near his recently established outpost.

The émigrés reached Pensacola around July 28, 1704. The wives and children of eight Spanish families from the San Luis region had already arrived by sea. Ivitachuco's chief had asked the governor to permit his wife and children to join the Spanish families evacuating to Pensacola by sea, but the governor denied his request. The Apalachee immigrants encountered a yellow fever epidemic in Mobile that sharply reduced their numbers. When the disease spread to the Apalachee settlements, they began to bring their sick children to the French fort for baptism. The first baptism recorded for the newly created French parish at Mobile on September 6, 1704, was that of a young Apalachee child. Its new parish priest, Father Alexander Huvé, had also contracted yellow fever along with the other two priests then in Mobile, and he was not enthusiastic about this sudden increase in the number of his parishioners.

Despite those and other difficulties encountered at Mobile, the Apalachee were sufficiently content there. They resisted coaxing from Pensacola's authorities to induce them to return to Spanish territory. By mid-1706, the Apalachee and Chacato who had initially remained in the vicinity of Pensacola had also migrated to Mobile. They informed the Spanish authorities that the French assisted them better than the Spaniards did and even furnished them with firearms. They reminded the Spanish commander that their wives were subjected to sexual abuse among the Spaniards but that they were safe among the French.

THE NORTHWARD MIGRATION

The Apalachee émigrés, free and slave, who headed northeastward with Moore toward South Carolina or northward to settle among the Creek, represented the largest contingent by far. Almost nothing is known about the fate of those who were enslaved. Most adult males probably were sold out of the region quickly to lessen the likelihood of flight. Those captured at the Flint River ambush in late 1702 were the subject of political deliberations. The lower house of the colonial assembly in January 1704 voted down a motion to sell them as slaves, probably in the hope of winning over the many Apalachee in Spanish territory known to be deeply dissatisfied with the Spanish government. The majority of the free immigrants were settled in three or four towns in the vicinity of Augusta, Georgia. Because of the abuses they suffered at the hands of English traders, the Carolina Apalachee joined the general Indian revolt of 1715 known as the Yamasee War. By that time the free émigrés had been reduced from 1300 to 638.

Those who survived that war dispersed widely. Some settled among the Creek who returned to their Chattahoochee River towns. They eventually lost their identity as Apalachee, but during the years immediately following 1715 they formed the core of the pro-Spanish element among the Lower Creek. Some migrated to St. Augustine, as did many of the Yamasee, or settled near the fort that Spaniards soon built at St. Marks in Apalachee. Others settled near Pensacola; still others moved on to Mobile to join the Apalachee who had lived there since 1704.

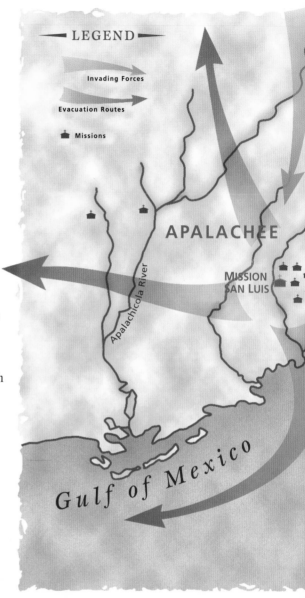

Map depicting the various evacuation routes taken by the Apalachee

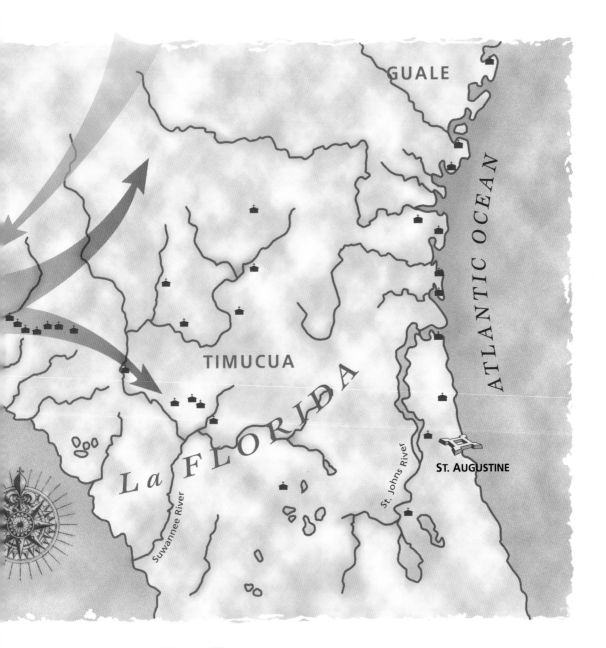

THE EASTWARD MIGRATION

The Apalachee who migrated eastward appear to have been among the least fortunate of the groups forced to leave their homeland in 1704. Before the end of 1705, most of those who fled while Moore's attack was in progress had been massacred in their wooded refuge in Timucua. Those who accompanied

Ivitachuco's don Patricio Hinachuba, who left with the Spaniards in July 1704, had an almost equally short and brutal life. He spurned the initial Spanish invitation to accompany the soldiers to settle near St. Augustine, instead reestablishing his village at Abosaya in Potano territory. The Apalachee at Abosaya soon found themselves under intermittent attack by Indians allied to the British and by their fellow Apalachee who had gone over to the Apalachicola. The Apalachee abandoned Abosaya during the winter of 1705–1706 and relocated in the vicinity of St. Augustine. They were distributed among several of the existing native villages but found no more security there. In April 1706, many heathen Indians attacked those villages in conjunction with rebel Apalachee, killing don Patricio and most of the Apalachee who were with him. The natives and their friars were forced to seek refuge close to the city, within range of the castillo's cannon. The rebel Apalachee who joined forces with the Apalachicola seem to have developed a special hostility against this group of their fellow tribesmen who remained loyal to Spain. Perhaps this was revenge for don Patricio's earlier refusal to support their plan to destroy the Spanish community at San Luis.

Some of the Spaniards from San Luis fared none too well either during the first years of their exile from Apalachee in mid-1704. Jacinto Roque Pérez and his brother-in-law Francisco de Florencia died only a few weeks after their arrival in St. Augustine. This suggests that an epidemic may have been in progress there, paralleling the one the Apalachee encountered at Mobile. The widowed Cathalina de Florencia, robbed of all her valuables during the voyage to Pensacola, was forced to depend on charity in Pensacola and later in Veracruz, Mexico, where she eventually moved. Ultimately she received a grant from the Crown in response to a 1709 petition. When Diego Jiménez was released from prison in Charles Town to rejoin María Magdalena in Cuba, his health was too poor for him to provide for his family.

Out of San Luis's Florencia family, only Diego and his brother Fray Claudio continued to prosper. Diego returned briefly to his old homeland in 1716 in the wake of the Yamasee War, serving as an interpreter for Diego Peña's mission to the Apalachicola country. In April 1717, Diego de Florencia took the widow of Simón de Argüelles as his second wife. By 1709 Fray Claudio had become provincial or leader of the Franciscans of Florida and Cuba.

A census taken in January 1711 revealed that the 400 or so Apalachee who moved eastward in 1704 with Ivitachuco's don Patricio or with the San Luis garrison had been reduced by at least 90 percent. The 1711 Apalachee village, known then as San Luis de Talimali, held thirty-one men, eleven women, and six children. There are indications that a few male Apalachee may have been living in other villages. The forty-eight people identified as Apalachee may have included immigrants from South Carolina, since a few Apalachee fled from there soon after their arrival. By 1717, the Apalachee village known then as Our Lady of the Rosary of Abosaya had shrunk to thirty-one people despite the return of more Apalachee to Spanish territory in the wake of the Yamasee War. But, as the 1711 imbalance between men and women had been rectified, this decline probably resulted from the departure of single men. Twenty-three Apalachee warriors lived in two Timucua villages in 1717. The Yamasee's village of Pocosapa had thirty-four Apalachee and Timucua warriors. But the continuing disproportion between the number of Apalachee men and women foretold the rapid loss of Apalachee identity. In the native matrilineal societies of Florida, the children of the Apalachee men would be identified with their mothers' people. When Florida was ceded to England in 1763, only five of the Indians who left for Cuba with the Spaniards were identified as Apalachee.

THE WESTWARD MIGRATION

The only Apalachee émigrés who were able to preserve their tribal identity were those who moved westward in 1704 or after the Yamasee War. Mobile still had a viable Apalachee community in 1763, which moved to Louisiana's Red River to avoid coming under English rule. A Pensacola community described as a mixture of Yamasee and Apalachee migrated to Mexico, settling in a newly created town north of Veracruz. When the United States acquired the Louisiana Territory at the beginning of the nineteenth century, all the surviving Apalachee

*The Apalachee Indians of Louisiana. Gilmer Vallery's children (**left to right**): Jilian (born 1902), Hertzog (born 1904), Melissa (born 1905), Virginia (born 1894), and Francis (born 1908). Francis is the mother of Gilmer Bennett, current chief of the Talimali Band Apalachee Indians of Louisiana. Photograph reproduced courtesy of Gilmer Bennett.*

were thought to have moved on to Texas. Their presence in Texas was last recorded in the 1830s. Recently Native Americans living in Louisiana have come forward claiming to be descended from the late-eighteenth-century Apalachee community there and are desirous of federal recognition of their identity as Apalachee. It is poignant to note that the new Apalachee chief and his family are still Catholic and have been able to document their tribal affiliation through parish records.

EPILOGUE

After 1704, Apalachee Province was never effectively repopulated by the native peoples who lived there from prehistoric times. Although some Apalachee were documented as living near the fort at St. Marks in 1718, none were listed in the 1723 census. The Spaniards who settled in the province during the mission period also had a limited presence in the region after 1704. Thousands of years of native occupation was brought to an end after less than a century of European contact.

APPENDIX
THE FLORENCIA GENEALOGY

The Florencia family tree contained within this appendix depicts the descendants of the union between Matheo Luis de Florencia and Luisa de Los Angeles and Gaspar Fernandez Perete and Francisca de Leiva y Arteaga.

**MATHEO LUIS DE FLORENCIA =
LUISA DE LOS ANGELES**

**GASPAR FERNANDEZ PERETE =
FRANCISCA DE LEIVA Y ARTEAGA**

| PATRICIO = MARIANA DE LA
M: 1625   ROCHA Y
          MENDOZA | LUISA = ALONSO DE
M: 1624 ARGUELLES | LORENZA
M: 1619
FRANCISCO
DE ALDERETE
M: 1627
JUAN RUIZ Y
CANIZARES | MATHEO LUIS
B: 1594 BORN AT SEA
M: 1617
FRANCISCA LEIVA Y
ARTEAGA | CLAUDIO = JUANA DE LEIVA
B: 1597   Y ARTEAGA
M: 1619   D: 1647
D: 1647 | FRANCISCA DE
LEIVA Y ARTEAGA |

THE FLORENCIA FAMILY OF SPANISH FLORIDA

- **COLOR 1 & 3** – DESCENDANTS OF MATHEO LUIS DE FLORENCIA AND LUISA DE LOS ANGELES
- **COLOR 2** – DESCENDANTS OF GASPAR FERNANDEZ PERETE AND FRANCISCA DE LEIVA Y ARTEAGA
- **COLOR 3** – DESCENDANTS OF PATRICIO AND MARIANA DE LA ROCHA Y MENDOZA
- **COLOR 4** – UNION OF PATRICIO AND MARIANA DE LA ROCHA Y MENDOZA
- **COLOR 5** – UNION OF MATEO LUIS AND FRANCISCA LEIVA Y ARTEAGA
- **COLOR 6** – UNION OF CLAUDIO AND JUANA DE LEIVA Y ARTEAGA

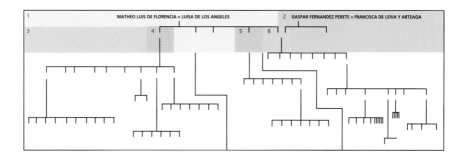

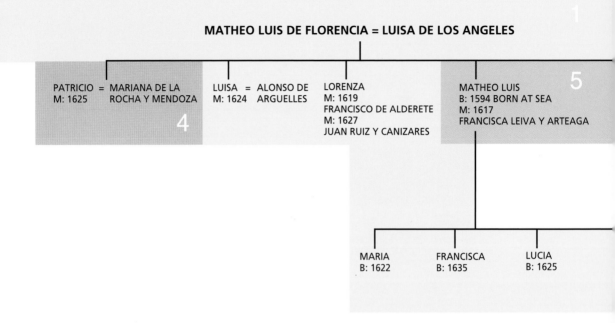

THE FLORENCIA FAMILY OF SPANISH FLORIDA

COLOR 1 & 3 – DESCENDANTS OF MATHEO LUIS DE FLORENCIA AND LUISA DE LOS ANGELES

COLOR 2 – DESCENDANTS OF GASPAR FERNANDEZ PERETE AND FRANCISCA DE LEIVA Y ARTEAGA

COLOR 3 – DESCENDANTS OF PATRICIO AND MARIANA DE LA ROCHA Y MENDOZA

COLOR 4 – UNION OF PATRICIO AND MARIANA DE LA ROCHA Y MENDOZA

COLOR 5 – UNION OF MATEO LUIS AND FRANCISCA LEIVA Y ARTEAGA

COLOR 6 – UNION OF CLAUDIO AND JUANA DE LEIVA Y ARTEAGA

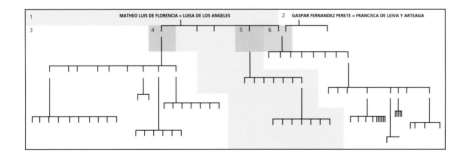

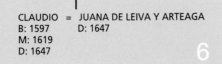

CLAUDIO = JUANA DE LEIVA Y ARTEAGA
B: 1597   D: 1647
M: 1619
D: 1647

6

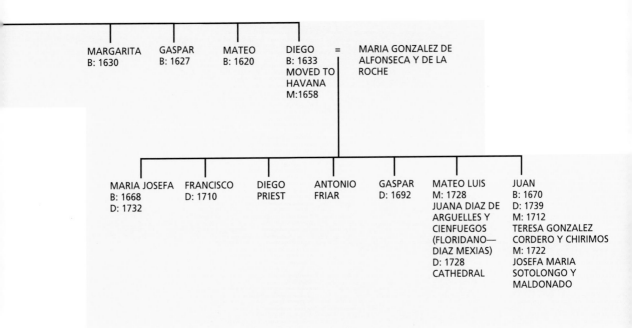

MARGARITA
B: 1630

GASPAR
B: 1627

MATEO
B: 1620

DIEGO = MARIA GONZALEZ DE
B: 1633   ALFONSECA Y DE LA
MOVED TO   ROCHE
HAVANA
M:1658

MARIA JOSEFA
B: 1668
D: 1732

FRANCISCO
D: 1710

DIEGO
PRIEST

ANTONIO
FRIAR

GASPAR
D: 1692

MATEO LUIS
M: 1728
JUANA DIAZ DE
ARGUELLES Y
CIENFUEGOS
(FLORIDANO—
DIAZ MEXIAS)
D: 1728
CATHEDRAL

JUAN
B: 1670
D: 1739
M: 1712
TERESA GONZALEZ
CORDERO Y CHIRIMOS
M: 1722
JOSEFA MARIA
SOTOLONGO Y
MALDONADO

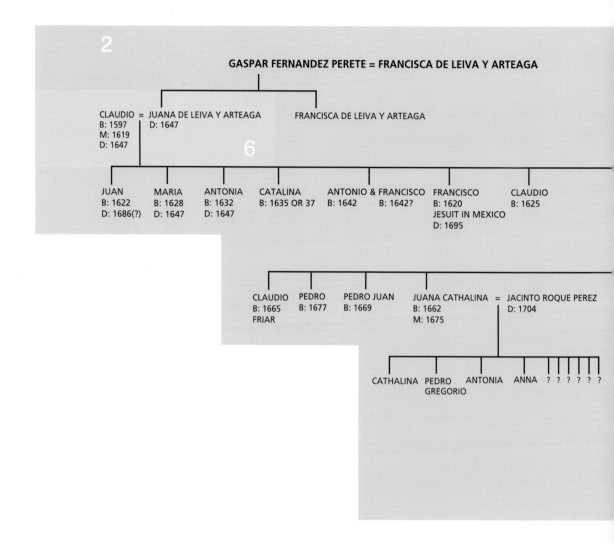

2

GASPAR FERNANDEZ PERETE = FRANCISCA DE LEIVA Y ARTEAGA

CLAUDIO = JUANA DE LEIVA Y ARTEAGA   FRANCISCA DE LEIVA Y ARTEAGA
B: 1597   D: 1647
M: 1619
D: 1647

6

JUAN   MARIA   ANTONIA   CATALINA   ANTONIO & FRANCISCO   FRANCISCO   CLAUDIO
B: 1622   B: 1628   B: 1632   B: 1635 OR 37   B: 1642   B: 1642?   B: 1620   B: 1625
D: 1686(?)   D: 1647   D: 1647   JESUIT IN MEXICO
                                                                                 D: 1695

CLAUDIO   PEDRO   PEDRO JUAN   JUANA CATHALINA = JACINTO ROQUE PEREZ
B: 1665   B: 1677   B: 1669   B: 1662   D: 1704
FRIAR   M: 1675

CATHALINA PEDRO   ANTONIA   ANNA   ? ? ? ? ? ?
           GREGORIO

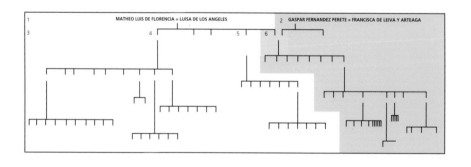

2

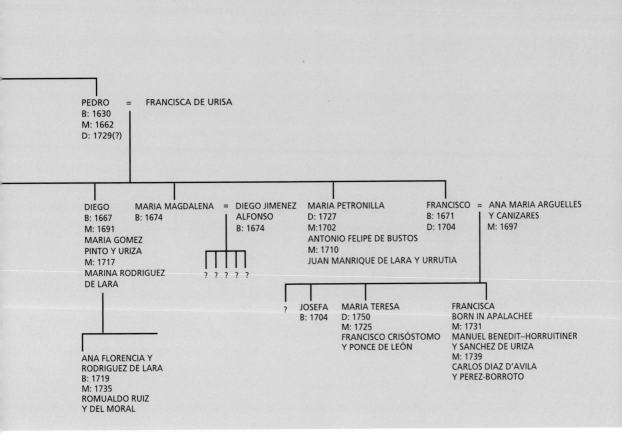

THE FLORENCIA FAMILY OF SPANISH FLORIDA

☐ **COLOR 1 & 3** – DESCENDANTS OF MATHEO LUIS DE FLORENCIA AND LUISA DE LOS ANGELES
☐ **COLOR 2** – DESCENDANTS OF GASPAR FERNANDEZ PERETE AND FRANCISCA DE LEIVA Y ARTEAGA
☐ **COLOR 3** – DESCENDANTS OF PATRICIO AND MARIANA DE LA ROCHA Y MENDOZA
☐ **COLOR 4** – UNION OF PATRICIO AND MARIANA DE LA ROCHA Y MENDOZA
☐ **COLOR 5** – UNION OF MATEO LUIS AND FRANCISCA LEIVA Y ARTEAGA
☐ **COLOR 6** – UNION OF CLAUDIO AND JUANA DE LEIVA Y ARTEAGA

3

LORENZA FLORES   = JOAQUIN (VISITOR OF 1695)   JUAN   ANA   CATALINA   JOSEFA
ILLEGITIMATE CHILD   B: 1638   B: 1640   M:1646   M: 1671   M: 1667
PATRICIO FLORENCIA   M: 1673   JUAN DE ASENCIO   ANDRES PEREZ   DOMINGO
Y FLORES   AGUSTINA DE LA   M: FRANCISCO SALVADOR   DEL VILLAREAL   DE AGUILAR
D: 1752   URRIAGA Y LARA   Y DE LA VERA

                  ROSA   ANA MARIA   ANA MARIA   JOACHIN   MARIANA LUIS
                  B: 1696   B: 1678   B: 1674   B: 1675   B: 1690
                                 M: JUAN JOSÉ DE   M: 1714
                                 LEÓN Y ARGUELLES   MANUEL ROLDAN

ANTONIO   FRANCISCA   JOSE   ANASTASIA   THOMASA
B: 1692   B: 1680   B: 1682   B: 1686   B: 1684

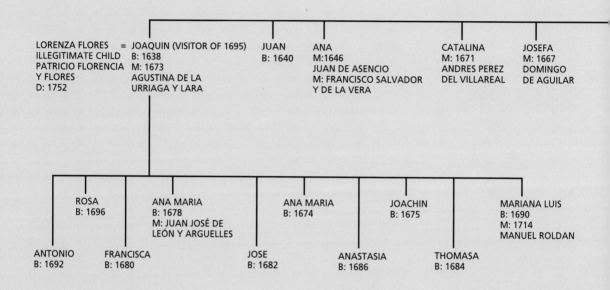

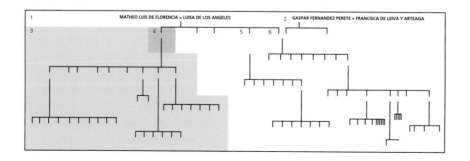

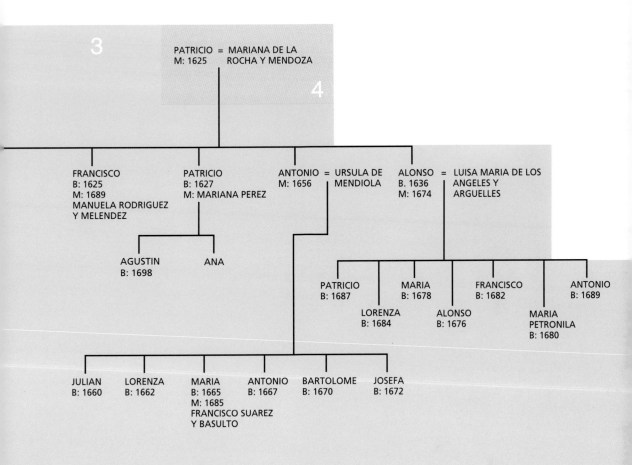

3

4

PATRICIO = MARIANA DE LA
M: 1625   ROCHA Y MENDOZA

FRANCISCO
B: 1625
M: 1689
MANUELA RODRIGUEZ
Y MELENDEZ

PATRICIO
B: 1627
M: MARIANA PEREZ

ANTONIO = URSULA DE
M: 1656   MENDIOLA

ALONSO = LUISA MARIA DE LOS
B. 1636   ANGELES Y
M: 1674   ARGUELLES

AGUSTIN
B: 1698

ANA

PATRICIO
B: 1687

MARIA
B: 1678

FRANCISCO
B: 1682

ANTONIO
B: 1689

LORENZA
B: 1684

ALONSO
B: 1676

MARIA
PETRONILA
B: 1680

JULIAN
B: 1660

LORENZA
B: 1662

MARIA
B: 1665
M: 1685
FRANCISCO SUAREZ
Y BASULTO

ANTONIO
B: 1667

BARTOLOME
B: 1670

JOSEFA
B: 1672

THE FLORENCIA FAMILY OF SPANISH FLORIDA

COLOR 1 & 3 – DESCENDANTS OF MATHEO LUIS DE FLORENCIA AND LUISA DE LOS ANGELES
COLOR 2 – DESCENDANTS OF GASPAR FERNANDEZ PERETE AND FRANCISCA DE LEIVA Y ARTEAGA
COLOR 3 – DESCENDANTS OF PATRICIO AND MARIANA DE LA ROCHA Y MENDOZA
COLOR 4 – UNION OF PATRICIO AND MARIANA DE LA ROCHA Y MENDOZA
COLOR 5 – UNION OF MATEO LUIS AND FRANCISCA LEIVA Y ARTEAGA
COLOR 6 – UNION OF CLAUDIO AND JUANA DE LEIVA Y ARTEAGA

Further Reading

Boyd, Mark F., Hale G. Smith, and John W. Griffin

1951   *Here They Once Stood: The Tragic End of the Apalachee Missions.* University of Florida Press, Gainesville.

Bushnell, Amy Turner

1994   *Situado and Sabana: Spain's Support System for the Presidio and Mission Provinces of Florida.* Anthropological Papers of the American Museum of Natural History, no. 74.

Deagan, Kathleen

1987   *Artifacts of the Spanish Colonies of Florida and the Caribbean, 1500–1800.* Vol. 1. Smithsonian Institution Press, Washington, D.C.

Ewen, Charles R., and John H. Hann

1998   *Hernando de Soto among the Apalachee: The Archaeology of the First Winter Encampment.* University Press of Florida, Gainesville.

Hann, John H.

1986   Demographic Patterns and Changes in Mid-Seventeenth-Century Timucua and Apalachee. *Florida Historical Quarterly* 64 (4):371–392.

1988   *Apalachee: The Land Between the Rivers.* University Presses of Florida, Gainesville.

1988   Apalachee Counterfeitors in St. Augustine. *Florida Historical Quarterly* 67 (1):52–68.

1990   *Summary Guide to Spanish Florida Missions and Visitas with Churches in the Sixteenth and Seventeenth Centuries.* Academy of American Franciscan History. Reprint from *The Americas* 46 (4):417–513.

1992   Father Juan de Paiva: Spanish Friar of Colonial Florida. In *Spanish Pathways in Florida, 1492–1992*, edited by A. Henderson and G. Mormino. Pineapple Press, Sarasota, Florida.

1994   The Apalachee of the Historic Era. In *The Forgotten Centuries: Indians and Europeans in the American South, 1521–1704*, edited by C. Hudson and C. Chavez Tesser. University of Georgia Press, Athens.

1996   The Missions of Spanish Florida. In *The New History of Florida*, edited by M. Gannon. University Press of Florida, Gainesville.

1996   *A History of the Timucua Indians and Missions.* University Press of Florida, Gainesville.

Hann, John H. (translator)

1986   *Translation of Governor Rebolledo's 1657 Visitation of Three Florida Provinces and Related Documents.* Florida Archaeology 2. Florida Bureau of Archaeological Research, Tallahassee.

1986   *Church Furnishings, Sacred Vessels, and Vestments.* Florida Archaeology 2. Florida Bureau of Archaeological Research, Tallahassee.

1993   *Visitations and Revolts in Florida, 1656–1695.* Florida Archaeology 7. Florida Bureau of Archaeological Research, Tallahassee.

Jones, B. Calvin, John Hann, and John F. Scarry

1991   *San Pedro y San Pablo de Patale: A Seventeenth-Century Spanish Mission in Leon County, Florida.* Florida Archaeology 5. Florida Bureau of Archaeological Research, Tallahassee.

Larsen, Clark Spencer, Hong P. Huynh, and Bonnie G. McEwan

1995   Death by Gunshot: Biocultural Implications of Trauma at Mission San Luis. *International Journal of Osteoarchaeology* 5:240.1–240.9.

McEwan, Bonnie G.

1991   San Luis de Talimali: The Archaeology of Spanish-Indian Relations at a Florida Mission. *Historical Archaeology* 25 (3):36–60.

1991   The Archaeology of Women in the Spanish New World. In *Gender and Historical Archaeology*, edited by D. Seifert. *Historical Archaeology* 25 (4):33–41.

1992   *Archaeology of the Apalachee Village at San Luis de Talimali.* Florida Archaeological Reports 28. Florida Bureau of Archaeological Research, Tallahassee.

McEwan, Bonnie G. (editor)

1993   *The Spanish Missions of La Florida*. University Press of Florida, Gainesville.

McEwan, Bonnie G., and Charles B. Poe

1994   Excavations at Fort San Luis. *The Florida Anthropologist* 47 (2):90–106.

McEwan, Bonnie G., Michael W. Davidson, and Jeffrey M. Mitchem

1997   A Quartz Crystal Cross from the Cemetery at Mission San Luis, Florida. *Journal of Archaeological Science* 24 (6):529–536.

Milanich, Jerald T.

1995   *Florida Indians and the Invasion from Europe*. University Press of Florida, Gainesville.

Payne, Claudine

1994   Mississippian Capitals: An Archaeological Investigation of Precolumbian Political Structure. Ph.D. dissertation, University of Florida, Gainesville.

1994   Fifty Years of Archaeological Research at the Lake Jackson Site. *The Florida Anthropologist* 47 (2):107–119.

Scarry, John F., and Bonnie G. McEwan

1995   Domestic Architecture in Apalachee Province: Apalachee and Spanish Residential Styles in the Late Prehistoric and Early Historic Period Southeast. *American Antiquity* 60 (3):482–495.

Shapiro, Gary

1987   *Archaeology at San Luis: Broad-Scale Testing, 1984–1985*. Florida Archaeology 3. Florida Bureau of Archaeological Research, Tallahassee.

Shapiro, Gary N., and John H. Hann

1990   The Documentary Image of the Council Houses of Spanish Florida Tested by Excavations at the Mission of San Luis de Talimali. In *Columbian Consequences*. Vol. 2. *Archaeological and Historical Perspectives on the Spanish Borderlands East*, edited by D.H. Thomas. Smithsonian Institution Press, Washington, D.C.

Shapiro, Gary, and Bonnie G. McEwan

1992   *Archaeology at San Luis: The Apalachee Council House*. Florida Archaeology 6. Florida Bureau of Archaeological Research, Tallahassee.

Shapiro, Gary, and Richard Vernon

1992   *Archaeology at San Luis: The Church Complex*. Florida Archaeology 6. Florida Bureau of Archaeological Research, Tallahassee.

Thomas, David Hurst (editor)

1990   *Columbian Consequences*. Vol. 2. *Archaeological and Historical Perspectives on the Spanish Borderlands East*. Smithsonian Institution Press, Washington, D.C.

Weber, David J.

1992   *The Spanish Frontier in North America*. Yale University Press, New Haven.

Worth, John E.

1992   The Timucuan Missions of Spanish Florida and the Rebellion of 1656. Ph.D. dissertation, University of Florida, Gainesville.

INDEX